Patterns of Time in Vergil

PATTERNS OF TIME

IN VERGIL

Sara Mack

1978

ARCHON BOOKS

HAMDEN CONNECTICUT

PA 6825
M28

Library of Congress Cataloging in Publication Data

Mack, Sara, 1939-
    Patterns of time in Vergil.

    Includes index.
    1. Vergilius Maro, Publius—Criticism and
interpretation. 2. Time in literature. I. Title.
PA6825.M28   873'.01   77-11704
ISBN 0-208-01694-5

Contents

ACKNOWLEDGMENTS

I must first express an indirect debt to Viktor Pöschl, whose book, *Die Dichtkunst Virgils,* helped shape my thinking on the poem long ago. I owe a great deal to discussions with various members of the literature faculty of the University of California at Santa Cruz, particularly George T. Amis, Harry Berger, Jr., H. M. Leicester, Jr., and G. B. Miles. I am very grateful, in addition, to friends who read the manuscript at various stages—to Maynard Mack for his unceasing assistance and support, to H. M. Leicester, Jr., for his excellent suggestions, which helped smooth over many a rough spot, and especially to C. J. Herington. Without his detailed suggestions and general encouragement this book would never have been finished.

Sara Mack
Chapel Hill, North Carolina
April 1977

I

INTRODUCTION

The theme, time in literature, fascinating and inexhaustible, invites study from various points of view. The subject has intrigued students of the novel, of course; it has also increasingly attracted those interested in earlier literatures.[1] Vergil's poetry figures especially in two sorts of study: in works of a more or less anthropological nature devoted to exploring time and time-related ideas in various cultures or various authors,[2] and in studies dealing with narrative technique, notably tense.[3] Each of these approaches is valid and useful, but each is limited. The first puts Vergil's handling of a theme like the Golden Age into a broader context, illuminating his practice from the practice of others. Such studies extract insights about time from his work, but they cannot, since their purpose is to generalize, limit themselves to considering a poem's use of time as part of its meaning. Studies of the second type tend to be limited in a different way. Examining tenses and studying their impact on the narrative is a first and very important step toward understanding Vergil's overall temporal strategy. But it will be useful to go further than is usually done, to link tense patterns with other temporal patterns visible in the poems and see what the general effect is. I shall examine various aspects of Vergil's management of time in the pages that follow and try to relate them to each other to determine a general pattern.

Some of the most notable differences between each of Vergil's works and its traditional "model" result from his special concern with time. This preoccupation with time is new in Roman literature, and we have to look far back in Greek literature to find a parallel. Greek poetry before the fifth century has very little

1

interest in the question of time, and thus time does not play much of a role in two of Vergil's models, Hesiodic narrative and Homeric epic.[4] The present is Homer's main concern, and he even draws into his present epic "moment" events that belong logically to the past—Helen's identification of various Greek heroes in the *Teichoscopia*, for instance, a scene which better suits the opening than the closing of a ten-year war. The future does not seem to interest Homer very much either. Predictions found in the *Odyssey* merely complete the adventures of the *personae*: e.g., Menelaus' life after death (IV, 561ff.), or Odysseus' journey with the oar (XI, 119ff). Prophecy serves a more dramatic purpose in the *Iliad*, keeping Achilles' approaching death and Troy's coming destruction before our eyes, but even this cannot be compared with the complexity of Vergil's usage.

Moving now from Homer to Apollonius, from early to Hellenistic epic, we find that the *Argonautica* is simpler in its treatment of time than are the *Iliad* and *Odyssey*. The past that Homer turns into the present, Apollonius almost entirely ignores. His few connections between a "then" and a "now" are usually aetiological, e.g., the incident involving Zeus and Sinope at II, 946ff. Though he relates these background stories with relish (rather like Herodotus), the connections he makes with the past are not morally loaded, not significant for the present, and therefore very different from Vergil's connections—those in Book VIII, for example, between Hercules long ago, Aeneas now, and Augustus in the future. In good storyteller fashion, Apollonius merely gives his audience the expository background information it needs.

His interest in things to come is also slight. The *Argonautica* contains a number of short-term prophecies that are fulfilled within the poem, like Idmon's prediction (I, 440ff.) of the expedition's success and his own death, but it gives us almost no information about the distant future. In fact, even its short-range prophecies deal most commonly with matters of no great consequence, or with characters who (like Idmon) are minor. Of the events that are to take place after Apollonius' tale ends (apart from the prophecy with which it opens), we could hardly know less. There is no hint of the well-known sequel to the story. One need only reflect how suggestively Vergil would have freighted that future with hint, prophecy, and portent to become aware of our ignorance concerning the fate of Jason and Medea after the *Argonautica's* close.

It is possible to find a parallel in Greek literature for Vergil's practice if we turn back to the fifth century—to tragedy, an art form which had considerable and obvious influence on the Roman poet. Time is a very important element in Greek tragedy, particularly in Aeschylus and Sophocles.[5] The action of a play can, of course, only depict the dramatic present, but the chorus and others refer frequently in their speeches to time past (or, as in Cassandra's vision, to time future). Aeschylus uses the chorus to create a past that in some way both causes and explains the present drama. Nearly all the important odes in Aeschylus' plays are concerned with the past, and frequently the glance back into the most distant past, in the center of the play, is joined with predictions of the future.[6] This is rather like the complex temporal web Vergil weaves (in the *Georgics* and *Aeneid*) with Laomedon's Troy at its beginning and Augustus' Rome at its end. In the *Aeneid*, past, present, and future are so carefully interwoven that they cannot be detached. Aeneas' mission would be incomplete without the story of Troy's fall and the hero's wanderings toward an ever-clearer goal: Rome, the real subject of the poem, would lack her beginnings. She would also lack the obstacles, the threats to her establishment implied in the all-consuming fires that are kindled in Troy, flame up again far across the sea in Carthage in the passion of Dido, and proceed, later on in the poem, to envelop the ships in Sicily, and, still later, in Italy, to engulf Turnus, Aeneas, and even the city of Latinus. Thus without Troy and the past, Aeneas would not be where and what he is; without Rome and the future, his labors would be meaningless.

In the *Aeneid*, Vergil does not ask us to regard the present as our paramount concern; rather, he makes us feel again and again that the present merely represents one step on a difficult path leading from the past to the future—usually a very remote future.[7] We know almost nothing about the events destined immediately to follow the *Aeneid's* end, only that the war will finally subside and that Aeneas will father a son, Silvius. The founding of Alba is the single event predicted for Ascanius. Otherwise we are told nothing of the fate of any character in the poem, although we hear a great deal about Roman history (the Trojans' distant future) in the events of the last centuries before Vergil's own day. The result is an interaction between what (for the story) is future and what (for the reader) is past. Fact and fantasy, historical and fictional time merge.

Such an interaction is effected in different ways in all three of Vergil's works. In the *Eclogues* it involves a unique blending of pastoral timelessness and contemporary Roman history. Pastoral always hides a city in its background, but Vergil brings Rome right into the pastoral world, and the resulting tensions give the *Eclogues* their special character. The *Georgics* is built on a movement back and forth through time which gives it a scope far beyond the limits set by its model, the *Works and Days* of Hesiod. Here too, one of the effects of Vergil's manipulations is to keep Rome, past, present, and (potentially) future before us. And finally, of course, in the *Aeneid*, one thousand years are brought together in less than ten years, as the legendary Trojan hero fights to establish the Rome of the poet and his Augustan audience. How very different this is from anything that preceded it!

If Vergil's preoccupation with historical and fictional time is new in literature, his treatment of it is equally novel and striking. He sustains no single temporal viewpoint in his works; he blends and shuffles times into elusive and changing patterns. Thus, time may often appear to be a linear entity marching relentlessly from past to future, as in the progression of cities from Troy to Carthage to Rome. So also Aeneas' stay in Carthage reaches out to embroil the distant future, for Hannibal arises from Dido's bones in the *Aeneid's* presentation of Roman history:

> exoriare aliquis nostris ex ossibus ultor
> qui face Dardanios ferroque sequare colonos,
> nunc, olim, quocumque dabunt se tempore uires.[8]
>
> (IV, 625-27)

> Arise from my bones, avenger, a man to pursue the Trojan colonists with torch and steel, now, hereafter, whenever strength will be granted.[9]

Elsewhere, however, time seems almost circular, like a globe spun before us, which we view from varying points—as at the end of

Georgic II, where past and present merge and blur, and the farmer's life takes on ever-changing meaning. Thus a single event may seem to mean one thing when we first meet it and something quite different later on. But some sort of pattern emerges as we follow Vergil's thought, a pattern whose shape we can perceive if we allow ourselves to be swept along accepting apparent discrepancies as part of the pattern instead of trying to explain them away.[10] Vergil's readers must strain their powers to see things as he does, that is, to perceive "patterns where other men would see only excrescences, digressions and eccentricities."[11]

This patterning works at every level. It is to be found in many details of style—the suggestive verbal juxtapositions, the ambiguous word ordering, the pairings of almost synonymous expressions (doublets) in which the second seems to resonate off the first—verbal characteristics familiar to all readers of Vergil.[12] It works in reticulations of motifs found throughout the *Aeneid*, most of them not specifically connected with time:[13] it also works in the telescoping of legendary and historical events. Take, for example, the extraordinary—in fact, surreal—compression of past and present in the *Aeneid*. Aeneas journeys only a few weeks behind Ulysses, as the Achaemenides episode in Book III shows, and thus has a temporal and literary connection with the *Odyssey*. Troy's first destruction (owing to Laomedon's treachery) occurred when Anchises was alive and living there; therefore the city's whole existence as Priam's great realm is spanned by one man's lifetime. In Italy, Hercules, the great civilizer of myth, killed the monster, Cacus, within Evander's lifetime: so myth blends with "history," as it does again in the circumstance that the Golden Age in Italy is just a few generations gone—Latinus is descended from Faunus, the son of Picus, who is himself the son of Saturnus. Thus Latinus is Saturnus' great-grandson and the Golden Age scarcely beyond the range of present memories.

What Shakespeare calls the "abysm of time"[14] is an almost tangible presence in the *Aeneid*. One way in which it is given a palpable being is by the succession of generations. Anchises, Aeneas, and Ascanius are, of course much more than father, son, and grandson; they are also Past, Present, and Future. The relation is, as always in Vergil, more than simply temporal—what it entails being made concretely visible in Aeneas' departure from

Troy bearing the burden of the past on his back and leading the future (whose guidance is solely his responsibility) by the hand. Similarly suggestive in the evocation of time is Pallanteum's royal family. Evander, like Anchises a very old man, represents the past, and his son, Pallas, the future. But the future for this family and city is doomed. That the city cannot survive as Pallanteum is brought home by Pallas' death (how inextricably the city is bound to Evander's family is suggested by its very name, "Pallas' town"); it can only survive if transmuted into Rome.

Past and future are entwined in the genealogies and backgrounds of other less important characters. Three of the four captains in the ship race in Book V are identified as far-off progenitors of well-known Roman families—the Memmii from Mnestheus, the Sergian line from Sergestus, and the Cluentii from Cloanthus.[15] In the equestrian exhibition, Priam looks back to Troy for his name and parentage (his father was Polites, whose death at Pyrrhus' hands is described so vividly in Book II); he also looks ahead toward Italy and the future, for his line will increase the Italian peoples (*auctura Italos*, V, 565). Atys looks toward Italy and Augustus' own maternal line, the gens Atia; while the Atian-Julian connection is clearly foreshadowed in the affection that exists between Iulus and Atys in the narrative present (line 569). Iulus' very name, changed from Ilus (I, 267), looks ahead, and his horse, a present from Dido, links the present with the recent past in Carthage. It would be possible to go on and on; we are unlikely to exhaust the *Aeneid's* supply of examples of this kind. One effect of this sort of attention to temporal connections is to make far-reaching expanses of time and space manageable and comprehensible to the imagination. Although Vergil alludes to a millenium or more, he does so in such a way that we can encompass it because he catches and consolidates his "battles long ago" in so many domestic patterns of human and historical relationship—"familiar matter of today."[16]

My main concern in what follows will be the *Aeneid*. I shall first look briefly, however, at the *Eclogues* and *Georgics* in order to give my discussion of the *Aeneid* a context and to see how Vergil deals with the problem of time in his earlier poems.

6

II

TIME AND TIMELESSNESS

IN THE *Eclogues* AND *Georgics*

In this chapter I shall look at some of the techniques Vergil uses to create a sense of time in his earlier works, the *Eclogues* and *Georgics*. With these in mind we shall be better able to approach the main subject of this book, time-patterns of the *Aeneid*.

-i-

The Eclogues

Perhaps the most notable difference between Vergil's and Theocritus' pastorals—the element that changes the very nature of pastoral—is the incorporation, in the *Eclogues*, of historical time in a timeless fictional scene.[1] My concern is chiefly with *Eclogues* 1 and 9, 4 and 6, and 10. In these, the traditional pastoral world, the timeless leisured Arcadia of poet-shepherds familiar from Greek bucolic poetry, comes into contact with the world of time and event, and Rome, with all the weight of her historical and political associations, looms over the pastoral scene.

In order to define the timeless world upon which Vergil imposes Rome and history in the five *Eclogues* mentioned above, it will be helpful to look briefly at the other, more "Theocritean" poems in the book. *Eclogues* 2, 3, 5, 7, and, to some extent, 8, limit themselves to a fairly consistent portrayal of the shepherds' world: an artificial, isolated, vaguely defined, "literary" landscape, uniting features from Roman Italy with the traditional pastoral setting of Arcadia and Greek Sicily, not to be located on any map,

7

since its consistency, as well as its value to the imagination, lies precisely in its imprecision.

The same imprecision characterizes the shepherds. They are all more or less Greek, have Greek names, and are thus linked with literary pastoral rather than with the realities of Italian sheep-herding country. There are, moreover, very few allusions to Roman actualities. Though Pollio, Bavius, and Maevius are named in *Eclogue* 3, it is in pastoral terms, one subject among many for the singing match; 8 is dedicated to a Roman man of action and poet (possibly Pollio[2] or Octavian[3]), but this is very loosely attached to the poem. Otherwise, these *Eclogues* draw on nothing external to themselves. The time in which they are situated remains as vague as the other details, and time's passage is scarcely noted—only in the 2nd does the day progress from the heat of noon to the shadows of evening. Equally static are the shepherds' lives. Their most strenuous activity is a stroll into a cave (5), the driving of a flock (3), or the search for a lost goat (7). A few other "labors" are mentioned but not portrayed—reaping and weaving in 2, and washing of goats in 3. In short, nothing *happens* in this group of *Eclogues* beyond the singing of songs. The distinctive pastoral peace *(otium)*,[4] is both their subject and their theme.

Differences appear as we turn to the group that is our main concern. The very first lines of *Eclogue* 1 establish the bucolic world's fragility, hinting at the existence of an ever-present threat to the *otium* at its center. The nature of this threat is not initially clear, but the opposition of repose and motion, poetic leisure and flight is clearly defined at the outset. Rome enters the conversation at line 19, at first invoked only as the home of the divine youth, but gradually revealed also to be the source of Meliboeus' difficulties, and finally, to contain a principle of discord that is the very antithesis of *otium*. The dislocation of pastoral life *(undique totis/usque adeo turbatur agris*, 11-12), the turmoil that contrasted so vividly with Tityrus' peaceful singing at the opening is now defined as civil discord *(en quo discordia ciuis/produxit miseros*, 71-72), inseparable from the life of men actually living in time. Meliboeus, it now appears, was forced out because his lands were confiscated. Thus by the end of the poem, all the usual pastoral vaguenesses have been replaced with specifics. We have an historical era—the late 40s B.C.; an historical place—northern Italy; and an historical point of departure—land distribution to soldiers. A new sort of pastoral seems to be emerging, where fact and fantasy are blended, and where shepherds, whose main concern was song, actually depend for their subject and even for their existence on politics and history. The City has invaded pastoral discourse, and the implications are as dramatic in their own way—

> ite meae, felix quondam pecus, ite capellae.
> non ego uos posthac uiridi proiectus in antro
> dumosa pendere procul de rupe uidebo—
>
> (74-76)

Come my goats, my once happy flock, come. It is not I, stretched out in a green cave, who will, hereafter, watch you as you perch on a bush-covered rock in the distance—

as the expression on the faces of Poussin's shepherds when they discover death in Arcadia: *et in Arcadia ego.*

We may well feel that the pastoral world is doomed once it has been breached by time, once statesmen and soldiers have been glimpsed in its neighborhood, even if at a distance; for the activities of neither are compatible with *otium.* For the moment, however, Vergil allows the two worlds to coexist. The beech tree is an oasis of peace, for the *present* moment is untouched by the disruptions of past and future lying on either side of it. Meliboeus, we know, has arrived only after troubles that will resume upon his departure, but there is still an hour's grace. Later in the *Eclogues,* Vergil will bring Rome right into the pastoral landscape, exploding it irrevocably. Here, the two worlds stand in uneasy alliance. The pastoral world may depend on Rome for its good and its bad, but it still has its own integrity in the present.

The 9th *Eclogue* is, of course, similar to the 1st, but darker in mood, and the bucolic world is shown to be even more fragile—its very survival in the face of new pressures from Rome is tenuous. (The 9th *Eclogue* is often assumed to be the earlier treatment of a theme reworked—and made more optimistic—in the 1st. But even if 9 was written first,[5] its location in the collection suggests that, in

Vergil's overall plan, it must be seen as a restatement of 1. What was fragile then, is more so now.) Whereas Tityrus in *Eclogue* 1 received more than he asked, now even the expected fails to work out:

> audieras, et fama fuit; sed carmina tantum
> nostra ualent, Lycida, tela inter Martia quantum
> Chaonias dicunt aquila ueniente columbas.
>
> (11-13)

That is what you *did* hear, and that was the story, but our songs, Lycidas, are as powerful among the weapons of Mars as they say the oracular doves of Dodona are, when the eagle comes.

Not only has poetic vision failed to influence political decision-making, the poets themselves have barely escaped with their lives. In 1, Tityrus was still engaged in creating poetry—*tenui Musam meditaris auena* (line 2); now the poets can no longer make new songs; they cannot even remember the old ones. Furthermore, although some of the themes (nymphs, goats, Galatea) suit their setting, like Tityrus' song for the lovely Amaryllis in the 1st, a political theme has also made its appearance. Poetry henceforward will have a public relations and propaganda function, will be used as a bribe—praise for Varus if he can save Mantua; or for Caesar's star, which has outmoded the old weather signs. Loss is much nearer at hand than it was in *Eclogue* 1—the vagueness there as to whether Meliboeus is leaving *before* the soldier arrives (his takeover is given in the future tense), or *after* is replaced by certainty—here the stranger has already come. Even song offers no relief—it is to be put off until later, whereas it was formerly the most pressing business at hand.

The specificity of this *Eclogue* contrasts strikingly with the other group, the "non-Roman" *Eclogues*, and even with 1. Many details that were left floating in 1 (specific only in comparison with the greater vaguenesses of 2 and the rest) become definite and more harshly real here. We know that the location is near Mantua rather than merely somewhere; that the new owner exists in fact and has already dismissed the old tenants: *haec mea sunt; ueteres migrate*

10

coloni (line 4). Meliboeus had to leave, but at least he was not forced to hand over his poor flock to a usurper. *Eclogue* 1 may imply, but does not name, Octavian;[6] *Eclogue* 9 refers by name not only to Varus, who is directly linked with land distribution, and to Caesar's star, but also to two well-known Roman poets, Varius and Cinna. Rome has, then, encroached on the pastoral world in all its aspects: its very survival depends on Varus, its subject matter depends on the city; its poetry looks beyond the boundaries of pastoral toward a "Roman" style, evidently seeking to compete with a poetry more urban:

> nam neque adhuc Vario uideor nec dicere Cinna
> digna, sed argutos inter strepere anser olores.
>
> (35-36)

> For, so far, I seem to sing nothing worthy of Varius or of Cinna, but to honk, a goose among clear-voiced swans.

The name Varus brings to mind epic (particularly after the 6th *Eclogue*); the name Cinna suggests neoteric verse of some kind. If Varius is indeed L. Varius Rufus,[7] we are perhaps to think of tragedy as well. In any event, the boundaries are visibly breaking down, and pastoral will not, it seems likely, long survive the pressures from without and from within. Yet, as in the case of 1, the two worlds can coexist because the pastoral present still holds— disruption surrounds it and affects it, but within the present privileged moment nothing more violent happens than a leisurely walk toward town.

In *Eclogue* 4, the pastoral present is enlarged to hold both the Golden Age, central *mythos* of the bucolic ideal, and the achievement that belongs to civilization and to Rome. In this conciliation of opposites, the poetry of lowly tamerisks *(humiles myricae)* blends with epic, the poetry of action and event. Vergil fuses these disparate elements in the person of a nameless boy who seems to represent a principle of concord, joining the Golden Age and Rome, Pastoral and Epic.

The new Golden Age is imminent and is linked with a specific Roman statesman and a specific time. Emphasis falls initially on its historicity—it will begin during the consulship of Pollio (what could be more Roman than so dating an event?). Under Pollio's leadership, all traces of crime *(scelus)* will disappear and lands will be freed from perpetual fear. The details suggest historical Rome and her influence in the world. The Golden Age is thus, at the start, fixed in time: it will institute a new phase in Rome's development and will wipe out the evil of the past. As in the Bible, which also opens with a timeless garden and closes with a timeless city, history has its sources and its end in myth.

Vergil's Golden Age changes to accord with the stages of its representative, the boy. For the infant, the earth produces, spontaneously of course, not useful crops for a farmer as in Hesiod *(Works and Days,* 117-18), but little gifts *(munuscula)* suited to a child. In the second stage, pastoral blurs toward georgic, and the products that normally result from hard work and careful tending—grain, grapes, and honey—begin to emerge, still spontaneously, leaving the growing boy free to devote his time to his education. Here again, two worlds come together. The young child receives a romanticized but nonetheless Roman education, learning the nature of manliness *(uirtus)* by example from studying both literature and the deeds of his own kin;

> at simul heroum laudes et facta parentis
> iam legere et quae sit poteris cognoscere uirtus,
>
> (26-27)

> As soon as you are able to read of the glorious deeds of heroes and the feats of your father, and come to know what manliness is,

while simultaneously the world changes to a state that is somehow pre-civilization in character, though post-civilization in time: the timeless garden and the timeless city both at once. While he learns his history, history is gradually unwritten; while he learns about civilization, civilization gradually disappears, beginning at the sea and ending with the plough. The cited examples suit eminently a young boy's age and temperament, for while he studies the merits and feats of the past, these are recreated for him in the present. Though lingering traces of past duplicity *(priscae uestigia fraudis)*, they are also heroic specimens worth of a schoolboy's admiration.

12

Finally, when the boy reaches manhood, the age for labor, labor itself will disappear from the earth and all trades with it. This consummation of the Golden Age involves freedom from impositions and restraints at all levels: the earth and the vine will not have to endure *(patietur)* implements, the ploughman will loose *(soluet)* the oxen from the yoke. The climax comes with the ram and the lambs feeding in the meadows in their lovely colored coats—wool will not have to be falsified with dye, what was formerly Art will now be Nature, and man's sophisticated tastes (the result of civilization) will be "naturally" gratified without his lifting a finger. Here is *fraus* indeed! Everything connected, however slightly, with civilization has been dismissed, yet the delights of civilization remain, and every land will bear all things in abundance: *omnis ferret omnia tellus.* (Contrast the *Georgics'* more realistic view of the impossibility of such abundance—*nec uero terrae ferre omnes omnia possunt,* II, 109.)

The poet concludes with the hope that he may live long enough to sing the boy's deeds *(facta). Facta* here, as in line 26, and *honores* (48) belong to Rome, as does the idea of *ruling* the world in peace (17). These have no place in the basic myth of the Golden Age, from which contest and struggle are exiled. To reconcile the timeless with time, Vergil seems to say, is to create a new kind of poetry—one that embraces the world of Pastoral (the life of the country—*rus*—the contemplative life of the poetic imagination) with its singing contests and its rivalries, its associations with Orpheus, Linus, and Pan, and also the world of Epic (the life of the city—*urbs*—the civilized community) with its emphasis on *facta* and *honores.*

Looking back to the beginning, we find that Vergil has prepared us for this fusion of poetic types all along. At the outset, of course, he states that he will heighten the bucolic strain slightly. The numerous allusions to Catullus 64, itself a short epic or epyllion, hint at a similar intent.[8] Furthermore, the lines concerning the boy's reading (26-27) suggest epic as well as history—*heroum laudes* being precisely the subject of epic. Lines 34-36;

> alter erit tum Tiphys et altera quae uehat Argo
> delectos heroas; erunt etiam altera bella
> atque iterum ad Troiam magnus mittetur Achilles,

Then there will be a second Tiphys, a second Argo to carry chosen heroes; a second time there will be wars, and once again great Achilles will be sent to Troy,

evoke both an heroic subject matter and an epic audience. Here the first one and one-half lines allude unmistakably to the *Argonautica*, the second one and one-half to the *Iliad*, which Catullus 64 assumes as its natural sequel. Vergil has succeeded in reconciling the two genres of bucolic and epic by coloring the subject of bucolic with the manner of epic (only to a degree, of course—the subject is *paulo maiora*, only *a little* greater), and the subject of epic, *facta*, with the manner of bucolic—for it is an Orpheus, not a Homer, who will sing. Thus in the poetry itself, as in its theme, Vergil extends the boundaries of pastoral to include both historical time (the poet's own historical present encompassing Rome and Pollio) and the very different sort of fictional time implied by epic.

Beginning with *Eclogue* 6, the pastoral world is opened up to the outside in at least two ways: by increased reference to non-pastoral figures whose names evoke historical Rome (Varus and Gallus in 6, the Romanized hero, Hercules, in 7, the nameless Roman in 8, Varius and Cinna in 9, and Gallus and Lycoris in 10); and by allusion to other types of poetry (epic, tragedy, and, in particular, elegy) alien to a strictly pastoral world. I shall consider only the first and the last of the group, *Eclogues* 6 and 10, which, taken as a pair, show us Vergil dealing with the question of time in a somewhat new way. (The 4th *Eclogue*, with its blending of disparate types of poetry, should, however, have prepared us for what we find here.)

Though many aspects of *Eclogue* 6 are still disputed, its concern with poetry and its neoteric cast are, I believe, agreed upon by all.[9] The poem opens with an apology for pastoral; it continues with a *recusatio* (another commonplace) rejecting mythological epic[10] and reaffirming pastoral. Proclaiming allegiance to Callimachus (through imitating the passage in *Aetia* 1 where *he* rejects epic), Vergil pastoralizes the Greek poet by changing "singer" to "shepherd," and "sacrifice" to "sheep."[11] He now addresses Varus, firmly opposing the bitter wars *(tristia bella)* of epic and the rustic muse *(agrestem Musam)* of pastoral. He has, then, rejected both mythological epic and "panegyric-historical" epic[12] in praise of Varus.

Why, then, if he has just rejected epic, does Vergil immediately set his scene in such a way as to bring to mind the *Odyssey*, an epic by the very poet Callimachus warned against trying to imitate? It seems likely that here Vergil rejects epic only to the extent that it cannot be pastoralized. Whereas a battle from the *Iliad* or a recent victory by a Roman general cannot fit into pastoral at all, certain episodes from certain epics are essentially pastoral or can be made so. From the *Odyssey* Vergil takes and rewrites the Proteus episode (also drawing on a tale of Silenus and Midas' shepherds[13]). From the *Odyssey* too he takes and modifies the Scylla episode, insisting upon the Odyssean component by referring to Dulichia, an island belonging to Odysseus' realm, in a seemingly different Scylla tale:

> quid loquar aut Scyllam Nisi, quam fama secuta est
> candida succinctam latrantibus inguina monstris
> Dulichias uexasse rates et gurgite in alto
> a! timidos nautas canibus lacerasse marinis.
>
> (74-77)

> Why should I speak of Scylla, Nisus' daughter, who, girded at gleaming hip with barking monsters (as the story has handed it down), ravaged Dulichian ships and tore up timid sailors in the deep whirlpool with her sea dogs.

From the *Argonautica* he takes Orpheus and his cosmogonic song, giving Silenus his attributes and his theme; from there too he takes the Hylas episode.[14] The theme of the beginning of this *Eclogue* appears, then, to be the nature and capacities of pastoral poetry.

The difficult question of Gallus remains. The presence of a famous contemporary Roman in the pastoral world creates conflicts, but here they are, as they are not in 10, smoothed over. Although it is certainly remarkable to find Gallus featured in Silenus' song between Phaethon's sisters and Scylla, his presence is, at any rate, several removes from "reality"; he is merely one subject in a song that is itself merely the echo of an echo, recreating

15

omnia, quae Phoebo quondam meditante beatus
audiit Eurotas iussitque ediscere lauros.

(82-83)

everything that Sparta's happy Eurotas river once heard while
Phoebus practised, and ordered his laurels to learn by heart.

Furthermore, only Gallus' role as poet is at issue. It may be that his
name alone brings to mind other connections, but the poem says
nothing about them, and, in fact, insists on the pastoral setting.
Gallus himself has no attributes, but Linus is a shepherd—*diuino
carmine pastor*—crowned with flowers and parsley; the reed pipe
(calami) he bears is, of course, a pastoral instrument; and Hesiod
with his pastoral-agricultural associations is equated here with
Orpheus, whom Vergil linked with pastoral in the 4th *Eclogue.*
Gallus is, in this *Eclogue,* substantially removed from time and
history as poetic successor to Hesiod. His place in the song seems
to indicate that chronology is not at issue. He and his kind of
poetry evidently fit, to some extent, into pastoral. Incongruities
remain, but pastoral can apparently embrace the sort of experience
represented by his meeting with Linus as well as elements from
older epics or neoteric short epics and narrative poems.

What pastoral cannot embrace, and what ultimately destroys
it, is the sort of experience and poetry that Gallus represents in the
10th *Eclogue* where he is an alien on two counts.[15] In the first place,
he is a Roman. This fact, played down in *Eclogue* 6, becomes
crucial in 10; Gallus is the only Roman to play an actual role in the
entire book of *Eclogues,* he is also, here, the chief character apart
from the poet. We find an authentic contemporary Roman in
Arcadia, and it is clear at once that he has no business there. The
poet has to remind him not to be embarrassed by the sheep, and
while Gallus himself at first wishes that he belonged to this world;

atque utinam ex uobis unus uestrique fuissem
aut custos gregis aut maturae uinitor uuae,

(35-36)

And if only I had been one of you, either guardian of your
flock or cultivator of the ripe grape,

16

and even tries out the shepherd's role, none of his poses is convincing. What makes his presence even more disruptive is that he is both a soldier—and no way of life can be more alien to the shepherd's than the soldier's—and also a love poet of the wrong kind. His songs are not pastorals but elegies, celebrations of a woman worlds apart from Amaryllis or Phyllis.[16] Nothing could be more unlike pastoral than Gallus' outburst as he imagines Lycoris' delicate feet treading the icy Alps far from her homeland; yet nothing is more congenial to elegy. There is a kind of elegiac frenzy about his attitudes in the poem, unlike anything elsewhere. No longer is pastoral an oasis with at least its own present integrity intact; it is shattered by Gallus, and the song sung now is wild and shifting. Elegy confronts pastoral, Gallus confronts the shepherd-poet, and elegy and Gallus are, finally, victorious. Apollo, Silvanus, and Pan, country gods, all try, but none gets through to him. Perhaps the speaker himself fails, for though he gives up pastoral for Gallus, there is no hint whether his love is reciprocated. At the beginning he asks who would deny Gallus songs: *carmina sunt dicenda; neget quis carmina Gallo?* and at the end (is it a wish? a command?) hopes his verses will be important to Gallus: *uos haec facietis maxima Gallo.* But what is Gallus' response?

As Pan suggests (28-30), extreme passion is out of place in pastoral (unless it has been fictionalized and, hence, distanced, like Pasiphae's, or comes to some sort of terms with pastoral peace, like Corydon's. It is, however, a trademark of elegy. As Gallus yields to love (*et nos cedamus Amori*, 69), the poet yields to his own love for Gallus (73-74), and pastoral recedes. The long shadows of evening, which in *Eclogue* 1 heralded repose and calm delight—with fruits, chestnuts, and cheese, at least for Tityrus—are now held to be dangerous and harmful for man, for beast, and for crops (75-76). The coexistence of timelessness with time, of fantasy with fact, is ended. The tensions left behind are resolved into a world of love and action that is wholly temporal, whose realities are of a different kind. This is the twilight of Vergilian pastoral, the poet calling his goats home at evening:

ite domum saturae, uenit Hesperus, ite capellae,

(77)

17

already hinted at in the verse from *Eclogue* 1 (when Meliboeus called along his unhappy flock), which this verse echoes:

ite meae, felix quondam pecus, ite capellae,

but only now, with the intrusion of real passion in an historical Roman poet, complete.

-ii-
The Georgics

In the *Georgics*,[17] time has a slightly different role from that in the *Eclogues,* but it remains an important vehicle for carrying Vergil's themes. Here we find (as we will in the *Aeneid*) not a confrontation between the timeless and the temporal, but a patterned movement among times: Vergil sets the present "moment" of the poem, with its emphasis on hard work and rustic simplicity, now against the legendary or historical past—Laomedon's Troy or early Rome, for example; now against the present embodied in Augustan Rome and urban civilization. The basic contrasts that we established for the *Eclogues* remain—myth confronts history, and the country confronts the city, each with its own type of poetry, here brought together by the poet who sings Hesiod's song through Roman towns (II, 176).

I shall limit my study of the *Georgics* to certain passages that exemplify the poem's characteristic movement back and forth through time.[18] Vergil's treatment, early in Book I, of the Golden Age theme familiar from Hesiod illustrates his method very well. The time structure in Hesiod is simple. Long ago there was a Golden Age. This was succeeded by an inferior age which initiated a series of ages, each worse than the last, culminating in the dismal present. Yet deterioration will continue until babies are born old—then Zeus will destroy the human race.[19] Having set his own age in this mythological setting, Hesiod deals with the way men, specifically his brother, Perses, should live in the age as it is.

Vergil uses the Golden Age theme in a very different way, coming back to it several times in the first two books. He presents it first as historical and past, describing its disappearance, initially to account for the destructive pests that blight farmers' crops,

18

ultimately to account for the rise of agriculture (and other trades). Except for the absence of farming in the Golden Age, which he describes positively (I, 125-28), he depicts not its qualities but the effects of its loss—venomous snakes, preying wolves, stormy seas replacing honey-bearing trees and wine-bearing streams; various trades arising to replace leisure. The invention of iron makes a fine conclusion to the list, anticipating the name of the Iron Age. Work won out, became the way of the world *(labor omnia uicit/ improbus)*,[20] he says in summary, then returns to the subject of agriculture where he began, with Ceres and the discovery of ploughing (147). He has come full circle. The Golden Age came to an end and gave rise to farming, at a point in time when acorns and arbutus failed and hazards of agriculture like weeds and thistles appeared:

> mox et frumentis labor additus, ut mala culmos
> esset robigo segnisque horreret in aruis
> carduus; intereunt segetes, subit aspera silua
> lappaeque tribolique, interque nitentia culta
> infelix lolium et steriles dominantur auenae.
>
> (150-54)

Soon distress came upon grain crops too so that evil blight consumed the stalks and the lazy thistle bristled in the fields. Crops die, a prickly forest comes up—burrs and caltrops— and among the gleaming rows infertile darnel and barren oats hold sway.

Thus immediately on its invention, farming is subject to troubles similar to (even if not quite the same as) those caused by pests like goose and crane, endive and shade, which were troubling Vergil's contemporary farmers thirty lines before (118-22). Then, in the process of listing agricultural disasters, Vergil takes us imperceptibly from the end of the Golden Age to the present georgic situation. *Robigo* and *carduus,* as the *ut* clause makes clear, are the result of the long-ago addition of *labor*. The other problems— burrs, thistles, etc.—brought before us by verbs in the present tense, seem initially to be no more than an additional series of pests (the change from perfect to present tense merely for variety),

but in fact they help negotiate our return from the long-ago iron
age to the present—the present tenses referring quite clearly to
now as well as to then, to the present as well as to the end of the
Golden Age, to the farmer's present problem with weeds as well as
to their genesis. What had to be done then has also to be done now:

> quod nisi et adsiduis herbam insectabere rastris
> et sonitu terrebis auis et ruris opaci
> falce premes umbras uotisque uocaueris imbrem,
> heu magnum alterius frustra spectabis aceruum
> concussaque famem in siluis solabere quercu.

(155-59)

> But if you will not pursue the weeds with constant hoe and
> frighten the birds with noise, prune back the countryside's
> shady growth and call on the rain in prayer, alas, you will
> look in vain on the abundant heap of someone else, and shake
> the oak in the woods to solace your hunger.

This warning about acorns expresses vividly the barrenness
resulting from laziness in a world that demands industry; it also
renews a theme indicated ten lines before, turning a positive
attribute of the past into a negative attribute of the present. There
acorns were produced spontaneously for men by a bounteous
earth, and their failure marked the ending of one age, the
beginning of another. Now they represent a poor substitute for
grain. An emblem of ease and freedom from toil in the past has
become an emblem of failure in the present.

The consequence of these manipulations should be, I think,
to jolt the reader from his contemplation of seemingly past events
and make him look at the *present* with new eyes.[21] Our perspective
is suddenly and forcibly changed as we read. What seemed to be the
distant past—Golden Age followed by Iron Age—is revealed as
being involved in our own present, and the Iron Age of myth blurs
into our own iron age, whose problems are the problems of old. As
a result of this blurring, the Golden Age, that enchanted,
irrecoverable time, while still past, no longer seems to belong to a
past so distant as to be unconnected with our own concerns, but to
be just out of our grasp, just around the corner, a backdrop for the

20

present against which we can measure it. (Thus acorns mean one thing in the old context, another in the new.) In addition, the present georgic situation, because it has roots in the distant past—the Iron Age *then* being the nature of things *now*—is at once easier and harder to bear. On the one hand, since Jupiter's decree calls for unceasing labor, it is a burden without hope. On the other hand, since toil is thus known to be the way of the world, the burden, though heavy, is shared. Any sort of community of experience encourages, for labor shared is never so hard as labor that seems uniquely one's own. Thus Vergil's temporal manipulations have greatly enriched the topic under discussion. He has broadened our perspectives, making us see the farmer's life with new eyes, perceive his labors as more intimately connected with our own concerns than we would have otherwise.

After a brief exposition of the weapons the farmer has in his "war" against the land—*dicendum et quae sint duris agrestibus arma* (160)—Vergil moves on to discuss days and signs, concluding with a fantastic medley that ranges over weather signs, particularly those given by the sun, Caesar's death, civil war, and expectations for the future (438ff.). Here again he deals with the present in terms of the past, but this time in very pessimistic terms, with no rays of sunlight from a Golden Age in the past and little hope from the future. The farmer's world (like Meliboeus') has now been penetrated from without by a significant historical event, the death of Julius Caesar. Vergil begins by advising the farmer to watch weather signs and interpret them correctly so that he may be able to do his work more efficiently. This is a standard theme—Aratus deals extensively with weather signs, Hesiod dates seasons by them. What Vergil surprisingly adds is the notion, inherent in augury and the taking of auspices, that informational warnings are given by the heavens, by sacred geese, or some other non-human agency. This mixture of ideas produces a remarkable passage that moves from physical to psychological storms, and from a morally neutral aspect of farming to an overall national guilt growing out of the distant past to contaminate the distant future.[22] Past, present, and future come together with the farmer as the fixed point. In the recent past the sun showed his pity at Caesar's death, the sky and the earth were convulsed by it. In the far future, engaged in his usual tasks, the farmer will come upon

21

war's leavings, its javelins eaten with rust, its empty helmets and enormous bones (493-97). Yet the prayer for Octavian that follows is a plea in the present for absolution of Rome's guilt, a guilt that reaches from a past as distant as that future, out of Troy, across the sea, long before the events even of the Trojan War—back to Laomedon's treachery (*Laomedonteae luimus periuria Troiae*, 502). Rome was polluted even before her founding (the reference to Laomedon at this point is very apt[23]). Then we return to the present. What is wrong with the present, it emerges, is the loss of the dignity of farming:

> tam multae scelerum facies, non ullus aratro
> dignus honos, squalent abductis arua colonis,
> et curuae rigidum falces conflantur in ensem.
>
> (506-8)

> So many faces of crime, the plough's deserved dignity lost,
> fields a desert, their farmers gone; curved sickles melted down
> to unyielding sword.

The move from farm to battle lines has destroyed the dignity that it is one of the purposes of the *Georgics* to reinstate, and the end of the book shows the dissolution of what the poet set out to accomplish when he prayed at the beginning (*to* the same Octavian *for* whom he prays at the end:

> da facilem cursum atque audacibus adnue coeptis,
> ignarosque uiae mecum miseratus agrestis
> ingredere et uotis iam nunc adsuesce uocari.
>
> (40-42)

> Grant an easy course, approve my bold attempt. Come, pity
> with me farmers ignorant of the way, begin and even now
> grow used to being addressed in prayer.

The weather signs reflect a total dislocation of the world, which can only be repaired by the farmer's return to his plough. And though the future holds a return to order on some long-distant day, that promise almost disappears in the chaos that characterizes the book's end:

uicinae ruptis inter se legibus urbes
arma ferunt; saeuit toto Mars impius orbe,
ut cum carceribus sese effudere quadrigae,
addunt in spatia, et frustra retinacula tendens
fertur equis auriga neque audit currus habenas.

Treaties broken, neighboring cities bear arms against each other; impious Mars rages over all the world, as when race horses have broken forth from the barrier and speed over the course; the charioteer holds the traces in vain; he is swept along and the chariot does not heed the reins.

Despite their seemingly different subjects, the passage we looked at from the beginning of the book and this one at the end share an enormous imaginative range. In each case, the farmer's life, insignificant though it may be in the face of the enormous sweeps of time and events that govern the universe, acquires, through the juxtaposition of past, present, and future, a moral force which is characteristically Vergilian—it becomes the mirror of the universe. The effect may be compared with the extensions (less commanding but somewhat similar) that Wordsworth achieves in the girl's song in his "Solitary Reaper," where he fuses in its background Arabia with the Hebrides, the desert with the sea, lassitude with energy, the past with the present, war with peace, epic deeds with ordinary mortal woes. The girl's song, like Vergil's farmer, gradually begins to create resonances in our minds that, strictly speaking, have nothing to do with it:

No Nightingale did ever chaunt
More welcome notes to weary bands
Of travellers in some shady haunt,
Among Arabian sands;
A voice so thrilling ne'er was heard
In spring-time from the Cuckoo-bird,
Breaking the silence of the seas
Among the farthest Hebrides.

Will no one tell me what she sings?—
Perhaps the plaintive numbers flow

For old, unhappy, far-off things,
And battles long ago:
Or is it some more humble lay,
Familiar matter of today?
Some natural sorrow, loss or pain,
That has been, and may be again?

(lines 1-16)[24]

We are left at the end of *Georgics* I with anarchy, all attempts at order and control having failed. In Book II Vergil restores the balance. Early in the Book, he returns to the Golden Age theme in a new guise. In the famous *Laudes Italiae* the Golden Age no longer gleams irrecoverable in the distant legendary past, it is depicted, rather, as the current condition of agricultural Italy:

hic uer adsiduum atque alienis mensibus aestas: .
bis grauidae pecudes, bis pomis utilis arbos.
at rabidae tigres absunt et saeua leonum
semina, nec miseros fallunt aconita legentis,
nec rapit immensos orbis per humum neque tanto
squameus in spiram tractu se colligit anguis.

(149ff.)

Here is perpetual spring and summer in foreign months. Twice are flocks pregnant, twice the fruit trees bear useful fruit. But raging tigers are absent and the savage seed of lions, nor do poisons deceive their wretched gatherers. And the scaly snake does not snatch his enormous coils over the ground or draw himself together in a spiral of such size.

The encomium grows out of the proposition that no land can produce everything and hence into a cataloguing of the treasures produced by the East, surpassed in every way by Italy. This is Vergil's most glowing and optimistic account of his homeland in the poem. Book II is generally more hopeful than Book I,[25] but even in this Book the passage stands out, for here and nowhere else, he grants Italy the elsewhere incompatible elements of Golden Age ease and hard-working progressive civilization. In the passage we looked at from the first Book the two were antithetical;

the civilization instituted by Jupiter was beneficial to man but destroyed the Saturnian age. Here there is no mention of the farmer—the various details suggest the situation before Jupiter, when agriculture had not yet been invented and things took care of themselves (although now the magical details are omitted). As in the 4th *Eclogue*, the Golden Age theme is joined with that of Rome and urban Italy. Italy, as imagined here, embraces both the war horse and the bull (the *victima maxuma*[26]), as well as Golden Age characteristics of eternal spring, inexhaustible fecundity, and absence of noxious beasts. To nature's abundance and man's ease, it joins the greatness of active men who build and conquer—the impressive military feats in the past of Rome's great families now matched by Octavian in the present (169-72), the eminent civilizing feats of the past—the many cities built on steep Italian cliffs (156)—now matched by the new Julian harbor (161ff.). This Italy is, to sum up

> . . . magna parens frugum, Saturnia tellus,
> magna uirum: tibi res antiquae laudis et artem
> ingredior sanctos ausus recludere fontis,
>
> (173-75)

Saturnian land, great mother of crops and of men. For you I enter upon matters of ancient glory and art, daring to open the sacred springs,

and the men referred to are clearly not farmers. Moreover, the poet who describes them combines the urban and the rural in himself; his song is Hesiodic, agricultural: *Ascraeumque cano*, but he addresses it to Roman town-dwellers: *Romana per oppida carmen* (176). The implication of Vergil's poetic statement at the end of the passage is, of course, that the city can learn from the country, not about the country's own *artes*, for these are nonexistent in the present view of the situation, but about the essence of the country, the possibility of harmony between man and nature.

The next passage I shall consider, the encomium on spring, is concerned with similar harmonies and is similar in feeling to the *Laudes*. It also has connections with the first Golden Age passage in Book I, for it is built on a similar movement through time.

Between the *Laudes* and the passage about spring comes a fairly straightforward discussion of types of soils and the best use to be made of each. At II, 226, Vergil describes the steps necessary to viticulture—kinds and treatment of soil, depth to plant, location of plots, and so on. He introduces the encomium with the warning that spring or fall is the proper season for planting vines (315ff.), then, ignoring fall, he describes spring, breaking into an almost ecstatic account of spring's fertility. It begins with sexual desire and receptivity—in the fields: *tument terrae, genitalia semina poscunt* (earth swells, demands generative seeds); in birds: *resonant auibus uirgulta* (thickets sound with birds); in beasts: *Venerem . . . repetunt armenta* (herds pursue love); and, finally, in vines: *sed trudit gemmas et frondes explicat omnis* (it puts forth buds and unfolds all its leaves). This general portrayal of fecundity then gives way to the distant mythological past, taking us back to the beginnings of the world, upon which the poet hazards the opinion *(crediderim)* that it must have been spring at that moment. The two springs merge; for the last lines apply to both, and thus ease us back to the present:

> nec res hunc tenerae possent perferre laborem,
> si non tanta quies iret frigusque caloremque
> inter, et exciperet caeli indulgentia terras.
>
> (343-45)

Delicate things would not be able to endure this task, if there were not such a long period of rest between cold and heat, and heaven's indulgence did not rescue the earth.

The world would not have come into being, the implication is, without spring, for it is its *caeli indulgentia* that allows all birth and growth. *Res tenerae* can be applied to all the newly arrived creatures, the herds, the iron progeny, the wild animals, and the stars—they are all new, inexperienced, and so in potential danger. But, *res tenerae* refers also, of course, and most specifically, to the young shoots of the vine, the topic Vergil left behind when he moved into the past.[27] He has proceeded step by step from their generation to early growth, and these final lines simply explain the need for spring's mildness at this point in their career—birth

26

and growth are difficult and would be impossible without a period between the cold of winter and the heat of summer. Yet seed time for vines, the topic under discussion, (like the reaper's song in Wordsworth), has been wonderfully enriched by Vergil's excursus into the past. Seeding now shares in the creativity of the springtime of the world; the farmer's labor has become a part of the nature of things[28] rather than merely unredeemed hard work.

At the very end of this Book (lines 458ff.), Vergil returns to the Golden Age theme for the last time and in this finale brings in elements from all the passages we have touched on. The passage has been described as a "rhapsody on the happiness of rural life...."[29] It begins with the good fortune of farmers—if they were only aware of it:

> o fortunatos nimium, sua si bona norint,
> agricolas! quibus ipsa procul discordibus armis
> fundit humo facilem uictum iustissima tellus.
>
> (458ff.)

> O too fortunate farmers, if they only knew their good fortune!
> For them the very earth, far from discordant arms, pours forth
> from the ground an easy livelihood, most bounteously.

Their good fortune lies in their being removed from battle and in the generosity of the earth, while their failure to realize their happiness derives, although Vergil does not make the connection at this point, from the simplicity of their life, a life that contrasts sharply with urban wealth and prestige. The farmer's world offers the advantages of a conscience at rest, sturdiness of character, and a penurious but upright existence far from the corrupting forces of wealth and influence. Among farmers Justice lingered longest as she departed from the world:

> . . . extrema per illos
> Iustitia excedens terris vestigia fecit.
>
> (473-74)

Justice! Once again, we become aware, Vergil has worked his special magic with our perceptions of time. The hardy moral people whose peaceful pursuits have just been described are no longer present-day Italian farmers, they belong to the legendary past when Justice could survive on earth with men. Justice— whatever her title: Parthenos and Dike (Aratus), Iustitia (Catullus 64), and Virgo (*Eclogue* 4)—belongs to the Golden Age when there was yet rapport between men and gods. Vergil thus equates here the farmer's present and his potential assessment of it (this whole description was, we remember, introduced by the conditional *si bona norint*) with his legendary past.

Next, the poet imagines a choice (as in *Eclogue* 6, a choice between kinds of poetry), here between a philosophical Lucretian sort of poetry and the poetry of country life. After an initial hesitation, he chooses (as he did in the *Eclogue*), the less glorious. But is it in fact less glorious? It is the poet himself

> . . . deos qui nouit agrestis
> Panaque Siluanumque senem Nymphasque sorores.
>
> (493-94)

> who knows the country's gods, Pan and old Silvanus, and the sister Nymphs.

(We think, perhaps, of *Eclogue* 10 where Pan and Silvanus appeared to Gallus, who saw them, but could not accept their message.) It is the poet himself who is unaffected by the madness of politics and empires, who possesses the Golden Age in his own life:

> quos rami fructus, quos ipsa uolentia rura
> sponte tulere sua, carpsit, nec ferrea iura
> insanumque forum aut populi tabularia uidit.
>
> (500ff.)

> He plucks the fruits which the branches, which the fields of their own accord have brought forth spontaneously, nor does he look to the iron laws, the mad forum or the public archives.

Quite suddenly, the Golden Age has become, not a time, but a condition.[30]

28

No longer, however, it is worth noticing, is there reconciliation of city and country, as in the *Laudes*. Here everything that
derives from the city is bad, the only good is in country simplicity.
Even sailing, which might seem relatively harmless in the context
of the greater evils described in the brief satire on city life (503-12),
is out of place. None of its pursuits is congenial to the condition of
the Golden Age. Meanwhile the farmer is at work ploughing, the
seasons bring their various products, family life is happy and
chaste. This is what the farmer's life is all about: constant work,
crowned by the wholesome delights of holiday seasons. But then,
with a quick reversal of the glass, Vergil puts all this far back into
the past:

> hanc olim ueteres uitam coluere Sabini,
> hanc Remus et frater; sic fortis Etruria creuit
> scilicet et rerum facta est pulcherrima Roma,
> septemque una sibi muro circumdedit arces.
> ante etiam sceptrum Dictaei regis et ante
> impia quam caesis gens est epulata iuuencis,
> aureus hanc uitam in terris Saturnus agebat;
> necdum etiam audierant inflari classica, necdum
> impositos duris crepitare incudibus ensis.
>
> (532ff.)

This is the life the Sabines lived of old, and Remus and his
brother, thus Etruria grew strong, and Rome became most
splendid of empires and made seven hills one, surrounding
them with a wall, before Jupiter, king from Crete, held sway,
before an impious people slew and dined off cattle; this was
the life golden Saturnus used to live on earth; not yet had they
heard the trumpet call, or swords clank on hard anvils.

This was the life of long ago—of Sabines, Romulus and Remus,
Etruria, early Rome—it is what made Rome great. This is the way
Rome was, not the way Rome is. Man was not then an *impia gens*.
This was the life of the Golden Age (in 538 Vergil states it explictly
for the first time), before Jupiter (and the beginning of all arts, we
remember from Book I), before the need for sacrifice[31] (when men
and gods could live in harmony and Justice resided on earth),

before war and arms-making (which appear to be the inevitable conclusion to the process of civilization).

All these shifts in time suggest much more than could possibly be stated by comparison of past and present or present and future. A single situation, the farmer's life, appears kaleidoscopically, presenting one aspect after another as it moves through time, and the farmer's life becomes the measure of the universe. Its order reflects an essential order in things—all too easily disrupted, but capable of surviving there longer than elsewhere—Justice may have lingered there but she did finally depart forever. We come away from the *Georgics* with a sense that something continually eludes man's grasp—just as Justice herself has retreated into the past, so our highest hopes and possibilities always elude us, receding into the past, as at the end of Book II, or even moving into the future, as at the opening of Book III:

> mox tamen ardentis accingar dicere pugnas
> Caesaris et nomen fama tot ferre per annos,
> Tithoni prima quot abest ab origine Caesar.[32]
>
> (46-48)

Soon, however, I shall gird myself to sing the fiery battles of Caesar and to carry his name in fame as far into the future as he is from Tithonus' beginnings in the past.

What Vergil suggests here in the *Georgics* is, of course, central to the *Aeneid,* a poem built on the notions of losing and leaving, and failing to grasp—the shade of a loved one, a homeland, or a golden future. Thus Vergil's earlier work foreshadows what is to come. Time races by, never to be regained:

> sed fugit interea, fugit inreparabile tempus.
>
> (*G.* III, 284)

To sum up, in both *Eclogues* and *Georgics,* time is a crucial element—in fact, we might say that it is above all the introduction of temporal complexities that makes Vergil's poems different from their predecessors. Theocritus may echo third-century Alexandrian concert hall songs in his 4th *Idyl;* he does not impose on his audience the specific historical dates and events that reference to matters like land distribution or Pollio's consulship creates in the *Eclogues.* Thus Vergil sets up a world in which timelessness yields to time, myth to history, the country to the city. In the *Georgics,* Vergil, like his predecessor, Hesiod, sets out to instruct his audience about the needs of the present and refers to the past to throw light on the present situation. But Hesiod only uses the past, specifically the series of ages, as a background for his precepts about the present, while Vergil blends past and present, so that times merge and shift and meanings change.

In the *Eclogues,* historical time is a theme implied in every reference to Rome. In Vergil's later works, time is incorporated in the very language of the poems, creating an additional temporal complexity. We observed earlier (pp. 19-20) how a present tense, which at first seemed a merely stylistic variant, could effect a transition from the original iron age to the present. In the *Aeneid,* this sort of tense patterning is fully developed and pervasive, and it is thus with an examination of its tenses that I shall begin my study of Vergil's epic.

III

Time and Tense in the *Aeneid*

The tense structure of the *Aeneid* is an important element in our perceptions of time in the poem; it is also surprisingly different from that of other Roman epics. Scholars have long been aware of something unusual in Vergil's handling of tense. As early as 1877 there appeared a monograph devoted precisely to that subject.[1] At present a number of good studies of various aspects of Vergilian tense usage exist.[2] The subject has not yet been exhausted, however. In this chapter I shall examine the basic pattern Vergil establishes through his manipulations of the four main tenses available to Latin verse narrative and look at some of the effects of this patterned use of tense. I shall begin with a rather technical study of specific details and then move on to a more general discussion of the poem's temporal structure. Readers who find statistics intolerable may wish to skip sections i-iii and read the summary of conclusions at the beginning of section iv.

-*i*-

It is necessary at the outset to establish the principles underlying the figures used in the following pages. Like Quinn[3] I exclude dialogue because I assume that tenses in direct and indirect speech are pretty much determined by subject matter. A poet writing about the past, may, however, choose to depict the action as past, or, ignoring the temporal difference between himself and his material, to depict it as present.[4] Unlike Quinn, who defines what he calls the "historic present" so as to include "description strictly within the narrative" but to exclude "dialogue, similes, flash-backs and other interpolations," I include all present tenses in the

33

narrative. None of these "interpolations" seems to me to be, in fact, separable from the narrative present. Therefore my counts include all finite indicative verb forms, excluding only the subjunctive mood, which is usually subordinate; the imperative mood, which is almost nonexistent in narrative; and the infinitive. The historic infinitive, as a nonfinite verb form, is, in my opinion, different in effect from finite tenses, even though grammars tell us that it is the equivalent of an imperfect. In *L.E.*, Quinn assumes four possible tenses: present, perfect, imperfect, and historic infinitive; he leaves out the pluperfect. (His counts leave out the infinitive as well, presumably because it is, as he says, rare.) Elsewhere, he includes the pluperfect as a possible tense but dismisses it as uninteresting.[5] He gives figures (in *L.E.*) for only one book, Book V. If one may judge from such a small sample as this, the figures that his method yields and those that mine yields are not unlike.

A striking fact about the tense structure of the *Aeneid* is the predominance of the present tense. This is our unmistakable impression in reading it, and the statistics of tense usage bear it out. Five books, chosen at random, yield the following frequencies for the narrative sections.

TABLE 1
VERGIL

	Book I	Book V	Book VI	Book IX	Book XII
	(Percent)				
Present	63.3	62.7	62.2	64.6	66.4
Perfect	22.9	27.7	26.9	22.1	24.2
Imperfect	8.9	7.3	7.8	9.3	6.1
Pluperfect	4.9	2.3	3.1	3.4	3.0
Future				0.6	0.3

It is remarkable here that the percentage of present tenses is so consistent and unusually high. True, the present tense is characteristic of the Latin language, not merely of Vergil. Every reader of Roman prose notices the "historical presents" of Livy and Cicero and is assured by the grammarians that "the Present in lively narrative is often used for the Historical Perfect."[6] Eduard Norden goes further and emphasizes that some predominance of the present tense is characteristic of Latin verse because of the difficulty or impossibility of fitting perfect indicatives (as well as pluperfect subjunctives) into meter in general and hexameter in particular.[7] We may grant all this and still acknowledge the distinctive character of the tenses in Vergilian narrative. Lucan's usage, for instance, is quite unlike Vergil's.[8]

TABLE 2
LUCAN

	Book II	Book IV	Book VII
(Percent)			
Present	56.6	55.0	50.6
Perfect	37.9	36.6	36.2
Imprefect	3.9	4.6	4.2
Pluperfect	1.6	2.7	1.8
Future		1.1	7.2

Plainly, though the present predominates, the difference in the relative frequency of present and perfect is not nearly so marked in Lucan's poem as it regularly is in Vergil's. Lucan relies much more heavily on the perfect, distinctly less heavily on the present (and also the imperfect) than Vergil. But perhaps this should not surprise us. We should expect Silver Age Latin to be quite different from the Latin of the Augustan Age. What about a near contemporary of Vergil? What about Ovid? Ovid's practice in the *Metamorphoses* is different from both Vergil's and Lucan's, but it is closer to Lucan's in the relative frequency of present and perfect.[9]

TABLE 3
OVID

	Book III	Book XII	Book XIII
(Percent)			
Present	53.4	51.0	52.1
Perfect	29.7	34.5	34.1
Imperfect	9.8	8.2	6.7
Pluperfect	6.4	6.2	7.1
Future	0.6		

In the *Metamorphoses* only about half of the verbs are in the present tense while approximately one-third are in the perfect—a marked difference from the *Aeneid*. Thus von Albrecht's statement that in Roman epic the presents are the rule, the perfects the exception, is misleading (although true), in that it obscures the special character of Vergil's tense usage.[10] Before moving on to examine Vergil's patterning of tenses, it will be useful to look at one last table, which shows the average percentage of tenses in the three poems, based on the eleven books I counted.

TABLE 4
AVERAGE PERCENTAGE OF TENSES

	Vergil	Ovid	Lucan
Present	63.8	52.2	54.1
Perfect	24.8	32.8	36.8
Imperfect	7.9	8.2	4.2
Pluperfect	3.3	6.6	2.0
Future	0.2	0.2	2.8

Thus, in the *Aeneid*, the average percentage of present narrative tenses per book is slightly under two-thirds, in the *Metamorphoses* just over one-half, and in Lucan slightly higher. The average percentage of perfect narrative tenses for Vergil is approximately one-quarter, for Ovid and Lucan just under and just over one-third respectively. Thus the differences are real and significant enough to be perceptible to an observant reader, as he reads, even though he does not, of course, count tenses as he goes.

What is most striking about Vergil's usage is the patterning of his tenses, and his practice seems to be unique. Norden comments that, in contrast to Greek, Latin frequently uses present tenses mixed with past.[11] This is true, but falls short of being an adequate statement of Vergil's practice. Julius Ley noted Vergil's patterning long ago and read it as a combination of a "relative" present, in which individual events are to be assessed not on their own, but in connection with things coming either before or after, and an "absolute" perfect denoting something special, of greater moment and great dignity, something that is outstanding in itself, either unusual in usage, or novel and unexpected.[12] According to Heinze, Vergil uses the present not mainly to replace a difficult preterite, but rather in such a way as to depict the occurrences as happening in the present.[13]

36

-*ii*-

To test these statements, let us look now at some passages from the *Aeneid*.[14] Its narrative in general is made up of blocks of "scenes," most of these developed paratactically, and drawing on the present tense. A typical example occurs early in Book VIII. The scene is introduced in the perfect:

> ut belli signum Laurenti Turnus ab arce
> extulit et rauco strepuerunt cornua cantu,
> utque acris concussit equos utque impulit arma,
>
> (VIII,1-3)

As soon as Turnus raised the flag of war from the Laurentian citadel and the horns rasped their raucous call, as soon as he spurred on the eager horses and clashed his arms, . . .

The scene itself, with its two parts—the actions of Turnus and the Italians, and the reactions of Aeneas—is in the present:

> extemplo turbati animi, simul omne tumultu
> coniurat trepido Latium saeuitque iuuentus
> effera. ductores primi Messapus et Vfens
> contemptorque deum Mezentius undique cogunt
> auxilia et latos uastant cultoribus agros.
> mittitur et magni Venulus Diomedis ad urbem
>
> .   .   .   .
>
>   Talia per Latium. quae Laomedontius heros
> cuncta uidens magno curarum fluctuat aestu,
> atque animum nunc huc celerem nunc diuidit illuc
> in partisque rapit uarias perque omnia uersat.
>
> (VIII, 4-9, 18-21)

Straightway spirits are excited, at once all Latium swears the oath with trembling tumult and the wild youth rage. The chief leaders Messapus and Ufens, and Mezentius, despiser of the gods, gather their forces from all sides and plunder the broad fields of their cultivators. And Venulus is sent to the city

of great Diomedes. . . . Such the situation in Latium. The
hero, Laomedon's heir, seeing all this, hesitates, caught in a
seething eddy of worries; now here, now there, everywhere he
divides and hurls his swift thoughts; they rove through every
possibility.

Thus the connections, explanations, and motivations—the sig-
nal, horses and arms—are given in the perfect, while all the
essentials of the "plot"—the mustering of the Latin forces, the
message to Diomedes, Aeneas' concern with what he sees around
him—are set out in the present.

One immediately visible consequence of this arrangement of
tenses is that the distinction between present and perfect becomes
more than merely temporal, although, of course, temporal connotations remain. The four perfect tenses at the outset (reading
turbati as an adjective) are temporally subordinate in that they
show what happened before the main actions begin; they show
something that is finished. The present tenses show something in
process. The perfects are also syntactically subordinate in that they
suggest the cause for the main statement in the present. Thus the
present tenses describe what is happening, the perfect tenses give
the circumstances or grounds of that happening. This distinction
is further sharpened by a marked shift in pace. Four perfect action
verbs occurring in two lines communicate a sense of movement, of
hurry emphasized by the repeated *ut* (as soon as), as if the actions
had happened almost at once. Then follow twenty-two lines of
present tense description, more linear and leisurely in construction, slowed down by verbless clumps of adjectives and nouns (and
by eight lines of dependent clauses in the subjunctive).[15] In the
passage as a whole, the perspective of the perfect tense seems to
offer a hurried glimpse of actions past, out of which, and as a
consequence of which, actions present lingeringly unfold.

An effect basically similar, although different in detail, may
be studied in the next scene, lines 26-67. The difference arises from
the fact that the substance of the scene is discourse rather than
narrative. Tiber's speech, beginning at line 36, a prophecy for the
future coupled with instructions for the present, is framed between
the perfects [16] that record his meeting with Aeneas;

38

Aeneas, tristi turbatus pectora bello,
procubuit seramque dedit per membra quietem.
huic deus ipse loci fluuio Tiberinus amoeno
populeas inter senior se attollere frondes
uisus . . .

(VIII, 29-33)

Aeneas, disturbed in heart by the bitter war, lay down and
gave his limbs late to rest. To him the very god of the place,
aged Tiber of lovely stream, seemed to rise among the poplar
leaves,

and the perfects that record his departure and Aeneas' awakening
(66-67). The speech itself is (in one sense) the equivalent of a scene
in the present tense, in that it, like the activity in Latium, is what is
lingered over; it is the important happening springing from the
circumstances instanced in the perfect—Aeneas' going to sleep
and the god's appearance. These particular circumstances are
essential to the situation for the speech, since it is, quite clearly, a
dream. In the dream, Tiber welcomes Aeneas to Latium and
promises him a home, then gives him a sign—the famous sow
prodigy—so that he will know on the next day that the river god's
appearance was not an idle dream, but a true vision. He then tells
him about his future allies, Evander and the Arcadians in Etruria.
The lines following this speech,

dixit, deinde lacu fluuius se condidit alto
ima petens; nox Aenean somnusque reliquit,

(VIII, 66-67)

He spoke, then the river buried himself in the deep pond
seeking the depths; night and sleep left Aeneas,

serve both as conclusion to the Tiber vision and as introduction to
the next scene (again in present tenses), in which Aeneas will act
on the information given him. Tiber's meeting with Aeneas may
be viewed in one light as equivalent to a scene in the present,
framed by perfects, a common Vergilian pattern. Viewed in
another light, however, the whole episode (with its framework of
perfects) functions as an introduction to the action in the present

(like those initial perfects setting the scene in Latium). When the narrative present stops (line 25) Aeneas is still worrying about what he saw in Latium; when the present tenses recur (line 68), his mood has changed and he is ready for action based on what the river god has told him. Here then, as before, the presents show what Aeneas feels and does, the perfects *account* for what he feels and does. They establish a psychological foundation.

The narrative following upon the Tiber scene, from Aeneas' rising to his departure (lines 68-85 interrupted by a long address to the nymphs) illustrates another aspect of Vergil's usage:

> surgit et aetherii spectans orientia solis
> lumina rite cauis undam de flumine palmis
> 70 sustinet ac talis effundit ad aethera uoces:
>
> .   .   .   .
>
> sic memorat, geminasque legit de classe biremis
> 80 remigioque aptat, socios simul instruit armis.
>   Ecce autem subitum atque oculis mirabile monstrum,
>   candida per siluam cum fetu concolor albo
>   procubuit uiridique in litore conspicitur sus;
>   quam pius Aeneas tibi enim, tibi, maxima Iuno,
> 85 mactat sacra ferens et cum grege sistit ad aram.

He rises and, looking at the rising light of the heavenly sun, duly holds up water from the river in his cupped hands and pours out the following words to the skies . . . Thus he speaks and chooses two ships from the fleet and fits them out with oars while equipping his friends with arms. But see—a sudden and miraculous prodigy, a white sow with her white offspring has lain down and is glimpsed through the forest on the green shore. Worthy Aeneas sacrifices her to you, greatest Juno, placing her and her litter on your altar.

Here ten of eleven verbs are in the present tense; one is in the perfect. The juxtaposition is striking. Lines 81-83 relate temporally, of course—she lay down before she was seen—yet her lying down also relates to the scene situationally. The "scene" moves from Aeneas fitting out his ships and arming his men to his seeing the sow and sacrificing her (all in the present tense).

Though the sow's lying down is the necessary preliminary to her being observed (*conspicitur*), it is not part of the scene. The whole clause in the perfect explains the circumstances of her being noticed—her whiteness against the dark woods and the fact of her having lain down on the green shore so as not to be overlooked. The perfect tense here obviously stands once more in some sort of causal (not simply temporal) relation to what follows in the present tense.

The immediately succeeding passage shows Vergil explicitly calling attention to this causal relation:

> Thybris ea fluuium, quam longa est, nocte tumentem
> leniit, et tacita refluens ita substitit unda,
> mitis ut in morem stagni placidaeque paludis
> sterneret aequor aquis, remo ut luctamen abesset.
> ergo iter inceptum celerant.
>
> (VIII, 86-90)

Tiber smoothed his swollen stream all night long, and, flowing backward, stopped with silent wave so as to make a flat plane of water like a gentle pond or a serene marsh, and no struggle for the oar. Therefore, they hasten the journey begun.

It is introduced by statements of fact in the perfect (*leniit, substitit*) and purpose clauses (*ut sterneret, ut luctamen abesset*), supplying the causative idea. The first statement in the present tense points back to this cause by *ergo* (therefore). As a result of the perfect verbs, in other words, the present verbs happen.

-iii-

I shall consider in a moment some of the consequences of Vergil's ordering of present and perfect tenses, but it will be helpful to consider first some typical conjunctions of these tenses with the imperfect and the pluperfect. The imperfect, something "imperfect," as its name implies, describes past action perceived as in process,[17] suggesting movement from an unstated beginning to an unstated end.

41

In the *Aeneid* the imperfect tends to give background information, which does not have a direct causal connection with what follows, but explains the *general* situation.[18] A typical example occurs in Book IV:

> haud aliter terras inter caelumque uolabat
> litus harenosum ad Libyae, uentosque secabat
> materno ueniens ab auo Cyllenia proles.
> ut primum alatis tetigit magalia plantis,
> Aenean fundantem arces ac tecta nouantem
> conspicit . . .

> (IV, 256-61)

Not otherwise Cyllenian Mercury was flying between earth and sky to the sandy shore of Libya and cutting the winds, coming from Atlas, his maternal grandfather. As soon as he touched the outskirts with winged heels, he glimpses Aeneas building fortresses and constructing houses.

The background, the general circumstances, are presented here in the imperfect—how and where Mercury was flying. The direct causal connection with the present that follows is asserted in the perfect (*ut tetigit*) and the present contains the main occurrence (*conspicit*). A similar example may be found in Book VIII:

> forte die sollemnem illo rex Arcas honorem
> Amphitryoniadae magno diuisque ferebat
> ante urbem in luco. Pallas huic filius una,
> una omnes iuuenum primi pauperque senatus
> tura dabant, tepidusque cruor fumabat ad aras.

> (VIII, 102-6)

By chance that day Evander was making the annual sacrifice to great Hercules and the other gods in a grove before the city. With him, his son, Pallas, all the noblest youths, and the senate (rich in years but not in wealth) were offering incense, and the warm blood was smoking on the altar.

Again, the background—who the people are, what they are doing, and how they happen to be where they are—is assigned to the

imperfect; the direct causal connection with the present tenses of
the new scene, to the perfect:

> ut celsas uidere rates atque inter opacum
> adlabi nemus et tacitos incumbere remis,
>
> (VIII, 107-8)

> As soon as they saw the tall ships gliding in the dark grove,
> men silent leaning on oars,

and the ongoing events to the present:

> terrentur uisu subito cunctique relictis
> consurgunt mensis.
>
> (VIII, 109-10)

> They are terrified at the unexpected sight, and all rise, leaving
> the tables.

The imperfects thus set the scene in a general way, the perfects
motivate the action, and the presents designate it.

Occasionally a fairly long passage occurs in the imperfect, as
in the introduction to the shield (VIII, 424-38), where fifteen lines
of imperfects describe the activity before Vulcan's appearance.
(Normally the longest imperfect sections are four to seven lines
containing from two to five verbs.) These actions are not essential
for the narrative as it affects Aeneas' progress, but afford a context
for the making of the shield. As before, the imperfects set the scene,
perfects sum up the direct preliminaries quickly and concisely,

> . . . nec plura effatus, at illi
> ocius incubuere omnes pariterque laborem
> sortiti,
>
> (VIII, 443-45)

> And he spoke no more; they hastily leaned to their work and
> divided it evenly,

and the real action of the scene, forging the armor, follows in the present. In a variation of this pattern which omits the perfect, the imperfect and the present continue to perform their distinctive functions:

> dixerat. ille patris magni parere parabat
> imperio; et primum pedibus talaria nectit,
>
> (IV, 238-39)

He had spoken, Mercury was preparing to obey his great father's command, and first he binds sandals to his feet;

> iam grauis aequabat luctus et mutua Mauors
> funera; caedebant pariter pariterque ruebant
> uictores uictique, neque his fuga nota nec illis.
> di Iouis in tectis iram miserantur inanem
> amborum et tantos mortalibus esse labores,
>
> (X, 755ff.)

Now heavy Mars was dealing out grief and death equally on both sides, the victors and the vanquished were slaughtering and falling equally, flight unknown to either side. The gods in Jupiter's house pity the vain anger of both sides and the fact that mortals have such trials;

> Troes agunt, princeps turmas inducit Asilas.
> iamque propinquabant portis rursusque Latini
> clamorem tollunt et mollia colla reflectunt.
>
> (XI, 620-22)

The Trojans chase them, Asilas leads the cavalry. Now they were approaching the gates and the Latins once again raise a clamor and turn back the supple necks [of their horses].

Quinn calls this "Tracking Forward"—"the narrator moves closer to the events he is describing till the past becomes for him the present."[19] In each case the imperfects give subordinate descriptive information while the presents control the main plot line.

The special status assigned in Vergil's poetry to the perfect and imperfect can be seen more clearly, perhaps, in contrast with his use of the pluperfect—a tense relatively rare in the *Aeneid*, but still worthy of comment. Quinn dismisses it, but, in my view, its role is not to be ignored, if only for the purpose of completeness. Nor is the pluperfect by any means so rare as Quinn implies. As the table (p. 34) indicates, two to three percent of the verbs in every book counted are pluperfect, and it has a function, at least in Vergil's hands, that seems quite different from that of any other tense. The pluperfect appears to be strictly temporal. All it seems to register is completed time, either as the past for a perfect:

> uenerat antiquis Corythi de finibus Acron,
> Graius homo, infectos linquens profugus hymenaeos.
> hunc ubi miscentem longe media agmina uidit,
>
> (X, 719-21)

Acron, a man of Greek descent, had come from the ancient territory of Corythus, an exile, leaving behind the marriage unconsummated; when Mezentius saw him routing the center ranks . . .

> transiit et parmam mucro, leuia arma minacis,
> et tunicam molli mater quam neuerat auro,
> impleuitque sinum sanguis; . . .
>
> (X, 817-19)

The spear point pierced his shield too, light arms for one so bold, and the tunic, which his mother had woven of supple gold, and blood filled its folds;

or as the past for a present tense; conveying no sense of causality, it accompanies the present when only temporal connotations are needed:

> umentemque Aurora polo dimouerat umbram,
> cum sic unanimam adloquitur male sana sororem,
>
> (IV, 7-8)

Dawn had moved damp shade from the sky when thus she in
her sickness addresses her own dear sister;

postera cum primo stellas Oriente fugarat
clara dies, socios in coetum litore ab omni
aduocat Aeneas tumulique ex aggere fatur;

(V, 42-44)

When the next bright day had driven off the stars at daybreak,
Aeneas calls his companions to assembly from all over the
shore and addresses them from the height of a mound;

uix proram attigerat, rumpit Saturnia funem,

(X, 659)

Scarcely had he reached the prow when Juno breaks the rope.

That the pluperfect should be drawn in to oppose the present
when the contrast is wholly temporal (frequently, as in the first
two examples, simply marking the time of day) offers further
evidence that Vergil's epic perfect holds more than merely
temporal connotations, that *sol medium caeli conscenderat . . .
orbem/cum . . . uident,* (VIII, 97-99) (the sun had climbed the mid-
circle of the sky when they see . . .) is meant to convey something
appreciably different from the lines opening Book VIII discussed
above. The pluperfect, being "more than perfect," suggests the
completion of an action which, once it has been recorded, is no
longer of interest to the narrative.[20] The reader's attention is
directed abruptly away from what has just happened. The event is
now past and irrecoverable. *Exierat,* for example,

iamque adeo exierat portis equitatus apertis
Aeneas inter primos et fidus Achates,

(VIII, 585-86)

Already the cavalry had gone out through the open gates,
Aeneas and trusty Achates among the first,

nicely dissociates Aeneas and Achates (and, most tellingly, Pallas)
from Evander's collapse. Aeneas is not given to us as leaving but as

46

already and irrevocably gone, all the details of his departure having therefore become irrelevant except for the one fact that he *has* gone, taking Pallas with him. We find a similar example in Book XI:

uix e conspectu exierat campumque tenebat,
cum pater Aeneas saltus ingressus apertos
exsuperatque iugum siluaque euadit opaca.

(XI 903-5)

Scarcely had he departed from sight and was in the plain when Father Aeneas, entering the open pass, crosses the ridge and comes out of the dark wood.

Here the conjunction of the pluperfect and imperfect brings out neatly the "near-miss" quality of Turnus' departure and its folly. When it is just too late—when Turnus has already left and is in the plain—Aeneas, with the greatest of ease (present tense), sails through the abandoned ambush.

One last, rather peculiar, usage of the pluperfect is also worth a look:

dixerat, Herculea bicolor cum populus umbra
uelauitque comas foliisque innexa pependit,
et sacer impleuit dextram scyphus. . . .

(VIII, 276-78)

He had spoken when the two-colored poplar, Hercules' tree, veiled his hair with its shade and hung entwining him with its leaves; the sacred cup filled his right hand.

A more ordinary construction would be some equivalent of the common prose phrasing, *cum dixisset, uelauit* (when he had spoken he veiled), perhaps *dixerat, uelauit* (he had spoken, he veiled). In Vergil's formulation, the pluperfect makes the main statement, so that Evander's having finished speaking receives the chief emphasis. The perfects, the veiling of the head and so on, make up the secondary idea. Additional weight accrues to the conclusory effect of the main verb when its human subject,

Evander, becomes the object of actions done to him by inanimate objects in the *cum* clause. Evander as agent, the verbs seem to imply, has done all he will do; his part is done; the poplar and the bowl take over as the acting forces.

-*iv*-

In summary, Vergil's use of tenses is different from that of other Latin poets, specifically Lucan and Ovid. Statistics show that nearly two-thirds of all indicative verbs in the *Aeneid* are in the present tense. Comparison with Lucan and Ovid demonstrates, first, that this degree of predominance of the present tense is peculiar to Vergil, and, second, that Vergil patterns his tenses in a way that is not found elsewhere. Vergil's narrative units (like little scenes) are largely in the present tense and these portray the main action. Transitional and subordinate material of various kinds is given in the three past tenses, chiefly the perfect, which accounts for approximately one-quarter of all narrative indicative verbs. The perfect tense tends to give causes, while the imperfect provides more general background information. The pluperfect, relatively rare, offers abrupt changes of focus and scene. The scenes are in the present tense; they are introduced or concluded by necessary information given most commonly in the perfect, as the poet's imagination, like the camera, moves quickly toward or away from a particular scene. The general setting, as the camera moves slowly toward its object, is given in the imperfect. Abrupt switches from the present to the irrevocable past are made in the pluperfect. All this differs markedly from Ovid and Lucan, who use significantly fewer present tenses (one-half or so) and more perfect tenses (around one-third—see Table 4, p. 36). More striking than the difference in numbers is the difference in the ordering of these tenses by the three poets. Studying two passages from the *Metamorphoses*, and two from the *Pharsalia*, I discovered that present and perfect alternate more readily in Ovid and Lucan than in Vergil. Furthermore, the fluctuation of tenses is either unpatterned or follows quite a different pattern from Vergil's. Ovid's practice is somewhat closer to Vergil's than is Lucan's, but basically what we seem to have in both the later poets is a story of past events told randomly in the present and perfect, with no substantial division of function. Thus the effect is different from Vergil's treatment of his "scenes" in the present tense with transitional and subordinate information relegated to the perfect. In Ovid and Lucan, neither tense seems to carry the main narrative weight. (The passages I studied, translations, percentages, and discussion, may be found in Appendix 2, p. 95ff.)

We come now to the question of effect. What does the arrangement of tenses in the *Aeneid* accomplish with respect to our perceptions of the poem?

One important effect of Vergil's use of the present as the main narrative tense is, of course, that of engaging us in the action, allowing us to see it as happening rather than as having happened—"past action as actually taking place before the narrator's eyes."[21] Our engagement by these means involves a partial suspension of our sense of the pastness of the history. In other Roman authors, like Livy, the historic present occurs in fairly short passages, to break up and vivify a narrative written in past tenses. A reader never loses sight of the fact that Livy is writing of the past even though he occasionally writes in the present tense. Vergil, in contrast, writes as if the action were going on in the present, in his mind, and his own rather melancholy sensibility shows through.

The impact of Vergil's habitual usage may best be gauged from those occasions when, momentarily, the poet drops his mask of anonymity and speaks as an Augustan Roman, the implied present becoming that of the historical Vergil. Normally, it is only Aeneas' present that is emphasized, and we watch it work itself out in a sort of vacuum where the relation of his present to that of the poet is unspecified. But occasionally, without warning, the poem's continuing present identifies itself sharply as that of Augustan Rome and so requires a complete shift in our orientation. A striking example occurs in Book V in the description of the equestrian exhibition:

hunc morem cursus atque haec certamina primus
Ascanius, Longam ·nuris cum cingeret Albam,
rettulit et priscos docuit celebrare Latinos,
quo puer ipse modo, secum quo Troia pubes;
Albani docuere suos; hinc maxima porro

accepit Roma et patrium seruauit honorem;
Troiaque nunc pueri, Troianum dicitur agmen.
hac celebrata tenus sancto certamina patri.

(V, 596-603)

This type of riding, these contests, Ascanius was the first to
revive when he founded Alba. He taught the early Latins to
celebrate them in the way he did as a boy, and the Trojan
youth along with him. The Albans taught their heirs; from
them great Rome received them and preserved them in honor
of their ancestors. And now the boys are called Troy, the troop
Trojan, games dedicated to a sacred father and continued to
this day.

Just before these lines, thirteen lines of present tense (ten present
verbs) conclude in the famous dolphin simile. The next two lines,
596-97, quoted above, give first the object, then the subject of the
next indicative verb (with only the imperfect subjunctive *cingeret*
signaling a change in the sequence of tenses) and suddenly
Ascanius' future founding of Alba and the institution of these very
games has been accomplished. The point of view has become that
of Augustan Rome, from which the poet now looks back to the
beginning, which is Troy (*Troia pubes*), then slowly toward the
future by way first of Alba (*Albani docuere suos*), and then of
Rome (*accepit Roma*). All these entail the perfect tense, and when
the present tense appears again, as it does in the next line (602), it
no longer refers to the narrative present as it did seven lines before;
it refers now to Augustan Rome.

A very striking example, because it leaves out the intervening
stages, occurs in Book VIII:

sol medium caeli conscenderat igneus orbem
cum muros arcemque procul ac rara domorum
tecta uident, quae nunc Romana potentia caelo
aequauit, tum res inopes Euandrus habebat.
ocius aduertunt proras urbique propinquant.

(VIII, 97-101)

The fiery sun had climbed the middle circle of the sky when
they see the walls and the citadel at a distance and the few

roofs of houses, which Roman power has now lifted to the skies, then it was Evander's, a poor kingdom. Quickly they turn their prows and approach the city.

The Trojans approach Pallanteum in the present tense (*uident*); the perfect (*aequauit*) is the type translated into English with "have"; the *nunc* is Augustan present, and *tum habebat* refers to what has up to now been the present of the narrative. Though no verb in the present tense refers to Augustan present, the present that the poetry assumes is Roman Vergil's, not Aeneas'. This abrupt change of viewpoint takes place between two sets of present verbs (*uident*, and *auertunt, propinquant*) referring to Aeneas' present. With a wave of the wand Vergil has transformed (just as he did in the *Georgics*) the *persona* of the narrator and the audience. He has suddenly relegated his story to the distant past, revealed himself as an Augustan Roman, and appealed to his audience as specifically an audience of Augustans. The remark is not directed to Aeneas or Evander, nor is it about them; it is an aside to the reader. While Aeneas sees a scattering of houses (*rara tecta*), the Roman reader sees the future, but rather as his own present than as the future. He is detached from Aeneas, separated both by time and knowledge—knowledge that he shares with Vergil and that Aeneas lacks. The comparison, suggested by Conington with Ovid, *Fasti* V, 93-94[22] is instructive:

hic, ubi nunc Roma est, orbis caput, arbor et herbae
    et paucae pecudes et casa rara fuit:

Here where now Rome is, head of the world, were tree and grass, a few cattle, an occasional house.

The two passages share a theme, yet they are worlds apart in construction.

Later in *Aeneid* VIII, in the walk through Pallanteum (306ff.), there is another curious temporal blend. The initial verbs (after the imperfects which set the scene) are all in the present. Aeneas asks and hears about the kingdom's past (*uirum monumenta priorum*, 312). Evander is characterized as founder of the Roman citadel (*Romanae conditor arcis*) encompassing past, present, and future. He founded Pallanteum in the past, he is present ruler of it, but the present citadel is Pallantean not Roman. Evander knows nothing of an *arx Romana* and never will, nor can Evander as *Romanae conditor arcis* mean anything to Aeneas. Evander's significance to Aeneas embraces only the present and the past, his support now and their kinship and family friendship dating from long ago. Yet when Aeneas hears Evander tell about the past, the Roman reader apprehends Evander as the beginning of a chain extending to his own time.

After Evander has told Aeneas the history of the place from its earliest inhabitants to the time in which he speaks, the poet takes over and points out what they see. The whole scene is given in the present tense: *monstrat, monstrat, monstrat, testatur, docet, ducit,* 337-48. In the *persona* of Evander, the poet tells Aeneas (and the reader) about the landmarks in Pallanteum, but in the *persona* of an Augustan poet, he tells the reader more. For they see first an altar and a gate, a gate which Vergil's contemporaries called Carmental. The first verb, *monstrat,* refers to the narrative present; before we read the second *monstrat* we find (in a relative clause) *memorant,* also in the present tense, but this involves a dizzying shift, because *memorant* refers explicitly to Roman time. She sang (*cecinit*) in 340 refers to the past—whether Evander's as well as a Roman's is unclear—while *futuros* points to the future for Aeneas and Evander and simultaneously to the past and present for a Roman. Within five lines the reader has been presented with two different presents and a past as well as with a future which is no longer future but present.

What Aeneas and Evander see next is called a huge grove (*lucus ingens,* 342), which in their past (but in Aeneas' and Evander's future) turned (will turn) into an asylum. As a matter of fact, just to make the temporal situation more complicated, Romulus restored (will restore) it to this use (*rettulit*) from whatever different use intervened. Thus Aeneas' present and Roman past converge in the imagination, as they do again with the allusions to Lupercal and Argiletum (343, 345). These Vergil describes in the narrative present, but not without conveying, in this context, a consciousness of the Augustan present looking back into its past. The first two landmarks, the Carmental altar and gate and the grove, are viewed in terms of a Roman present, the second two, Lupercal and Argiletum, in terms of Aeneas' present. The immediately following Capitoline scene (*Tarpeiam sedem* and *Capitolia*) brings all to a climax:

hinc ad Tarpeiam sedem et Capitolia ducit
aurea nunc, olim siluestribus horrida dumis.
iam tum religio pauidos terrebat agrestis
dira loci, iam tum siluam saxumque tremebant.

(VIII, 347-50)

From here he leads him to the Tarpeian rock and the Capitol, golden now, formerly rough with woody brambles. Even then the awful sanctity of the spot would terrify the timorous farmers, even then they would tremble at the woods and the rock.

Roman time is introduced by *nunc*, Aenean by *olim*, but despite the change in appearance, the similarity between the two times is emphasized by the repeated "even then" (*iam tum*). The reaction to the place *then*, in the past from a Roman point of view, shows itself to be the same as that *now* in the present, also from a Roman point of view. Evander's explanation that a god, perhaps Jupiter, inhabits the spot accounts directly for Arcadian feelings about the place and at the same time gives an Augustan Roman a possible reason for his more sophisticated associations. The "then" and the "now" become one.

The importance of the scene, like the importance of Vergil's conflation of times, lies in what it does for the reader. Aeneas himself experiences nothing that is significant to him in seeing the landmarks of Pallanteum: he does not even know, apparently, that this is the future site of Rome. A Roman reader, on the other hand, has been invited to become aware of two presents, his own and the Aenean present that has "made" his own, the *then* existing in the *now*. For at the end of the scene the two presents literally become one. Aeneas and Evander arrive at their destination. A contrast between their present and Roman present lingers in the word *pauper*, but Vergil does not contrast these as he did in the *aurea nunc* passage. On the contrary, he compels us to see each through the other:

talibus inter se dictis ad tecta subibant
pauperis Euandri, passimque armenta uidebant
Romanoque foro et lautis mugire Carinis,

(VIII, 359-61)

With such conversation together they were going into Evander's poor house, seeing here and there herds lowing in the
Roman forum and elegant Carinae,

speaking as if the Forum and Carinae existed in Evander's day.[23]
Here, as in the description of Evander as founder of the Roman
citadel, the Forum and Carinae are spoken of as if they not only
existed in Evander's day but were before his eyes. His cattle are
lowing in the Forum, and what is more, he and Aeneas see and
hear them lowing there. Vergil has blended Evander's present and
Roman present to create a sense image which, by its very
incongruity, encourages his audience to apprehend how intri-
cately Roman past is contained in Roman present and vice versa.
The experience of "time" has been incorporated in a landscape.

It is in its potential for this sort of effect that Vergil's choice of
the present for the chief narrative tense in the *Aeneid* reveals its
brilliance. In no other way could he have maneuvered fictional
present and historical present into so suggestive a design. Were the
Aeneid written essentially in past tenses, with occasional historical presents for vividness, the confrontation of these presents
would be impossible.

54

IV

"ROMAN HISTORY IN THE FUTURE TENSE"[1]

It is time to broaden our field of inquiry, making the focus less technical, the perspective somewhat wider. A close look at Vergil's tenses established two very different standpoints from which to view the action of the *Aeneid*—ordinarily the reader is engaged in Aeneas' present, occasionally he is asked to observe that present in terms of *its* own distant future, *his* own present and past. A further temporal complexity remains to be examined—the future. Direct reference to future events occurs almost exclusively in discourse (there are only about eight future verbs in the whole narrative), most frequently, of course, in prophecy. Therefore I shall look now at the series of predictions that guide and motivate Aeneas and give shape to all Roman history presented in the poem.

-*i*-

An important element in the structure of the first eight books of the *Aeneid* is the alternation of future and present—the future given in prophecies, the present narrative depicting Aeneas' attempts to follow the directions given him in these predictions. The task of the present is to move toward the future and become it. No major action is taken in the poem that is not in response to some summons from the future, from Juno's harrying the Trojan fleet to the seeking of allies among the Etruscans. The present is never regarded as an end in itself; it is merely a step toward, an obstacle in the path of, something still to come. Thus in the opening of Book I all Aeneas' toils in the present take place merely to insure the city's founding (*dum conderet urbem*, I, 5). Not only is the present not an end in itself; it is, in fact, almost always destructive

55

and wrong. Where the present is not destructive, respite is brief or else misguided, as in IV before Mercury's appearance, VII before Allecto's appearance, and VIII in Pallanteum. In this way, the poem consists of a series of destructive present moments, in which Aeneas must attempt to move toward a right or constructive future, for it is in the future that all room for optimism lies. The contrast between gloomy present and more hopeful future is indicated in the very first prophecies that Aeneas receives, those of Hector and Creusa in Book II. Yet the outlook for the future is not unmitigatedly hopeful, as the Sibyl's prophecy in Book VI shows. In fact, a considerable discrepancy often separates the future as predicted from its present-time reality in the poem.

There are two futures at issue in the poem and two sorts of prophecy to express them. First, and most commonly predicted, is the immediate future, which is revealed in short and fairly limited prophecies, nearly all of them addressed to Aeneas. These prophecies are "directional" and educational, for the most part guiding Aeneas toward his destination by means of commands, instructions, and explanations. They address themselves primarily to the hero's personal career and so are largely fulfilled within the poem as each moment of predicted future subsides into the narrative present. The other future in the poem is the distant future centering on Rome from its founding to Augustan times. This is revealed in three major prophecies: Jupiter's to Venus (I, 257-96); Anchises' to Aeneas (VI, 756-886), and Aeneas' shield (VIII, 626-728). These deal little or not at all with Aeneas' personal future and so the present they represent for the most part comes to pass outside the framework of the poem. The future predicted in the directional prophecies can be compared with its present reality in the narrative present, and so indicate something about the nature of prophecy in the poem.

One fact that emerges from a study of these prophecies is that, although they are "true," in that what is predicted generally does take place, they are nevertheless in most instances a very misleading and incomplete guide, partly because they do not reveal all— as Helenus makes explicit (III, 379-80), and Anchises' unexpected death illustrates (III, 708ff)—but largely because they give no indication of the relative weight of individual events, so that the same occurrence may have one appearance when predicted and another when seen in the present.

The two prophecies addressed to Aeneas in Book II and the first two he is given in Book III are very misleading in their optimism. In them emphasis is on future greatness and the ease of achieving it. Hector's words suggest that struggle belongs to the past. He would have saved Troy had its preservation been possible. Aeneas' task is flight:

> sacra suosque tibi commendat Troia penatis;
> hos cape fatorum comites, his moenia quaere
> magna pererrato statues quae denique ponto.
>
> (II, 293-95)

To you, Troy entrusts her sacred objects and household gods. Take them as comrades of your fate. Look for great walls for them which you will establish finally when you have wandered the length of the sea.

Even the future verb *statues* is embedded in a relative clause—almost as if it were part of the command. There is no reference to the difficulties Aeneas will face in accomplishing this mission except what is conveyed by the participle *pererrato*. Creusa, for her part, lingers on the aspects of Italy that make it ideal for founding a city. The land is rich (good for farming), it is already inhabited (facilitating settlement), and there a river flows gently (easy water supply and transport). They are ready and waiting for Aeneas— *parta tibi.* The *Aeneid* would be a very different poem if the actual situation closely resembled the predicted situation. All that is predicted happens, or will happen just after the poem's end, but, in entirely suppressing the cost, the struggles Aeneas will face, the prophecy is so oversimplified as to become the vehicle of a terrible irony not fully revealed until the poem ends. It takes six books and many years for Aeneas even to reach Italy, and once he is there, all the things Creusa promised turn out to be further obstacles in his path, leaving him in a worse postion than before. The presence of men and rich fields leads to an exhausting war and the direct cause of that war is the kingdom and royal bride, so casually coupled by Creusa with prosperity *(res laetae)* as the culmination of Aeneas' good fortune. Even when the poem ends all of these remain well in the future, though the way may at last be open to acquire them.

An equal irony marks the contrast between what Apollo predicts and what occurs in the present. Apollo orders:

> . . . antiquam exquirite matrem.
> hic domus Aeneae cunctis dominabitur oris
> et nati natorum et qui nascentur ab illis.

(III, 96-98)

Seek out your ancient mother. Here the house of Aeneas will dominate all shores, their sons' sons, and those who will be born from them.

He offers future dominion, to follow with ease and as a matter of course upon the Trojans' finding their motherland—the present that realizes this prediction offers plague. Since the plague is the result of Anchises' error in interpreting Crete as the ancient mother, the second and deeper irony of the prophecy is not evident until Book VII, when the true mother welcomes her children home—with a war, a war that is essentially a civil war, a war that never actually ends within the poem's narrative present.

Anchises' error is corrected by the Penates, and for a moment the Trojans' problems appear to be over. This is the last time that the future looks good. A slight hint of difficulties to come, in the reference to the long labor of flight (*fugae . . . laborem*, III, 160), is closely linked with the preceding statement of future fame and power and immediately followed by the explanation of Anchises' mistake so that it passes almost unnoticed. The Trojans set off joyfully; within five lines of their departure they are overwhelmed by a storm. The storm marks the beginning of the second stage of the Trojans' progress. In the first they did not know their destination (*incerti quo fata ferant*, III, 7) and so made random and futile attempts at settlement; in the second they know where they are to go but are unable to get there. When Aeneas was on the wrong course early in the Book he had no trouble with the journey. With great ease he reaches both Thrace,

> . . . feror huc et litore curuo
> moenia prima loco . . .

(III, 16-17)

I am carried here and establish our first walls on the curved shore,

and Crete:

> prosequitur surgens a puppi uentus euntis,
> et tandem antiquis Curetum adlabimur oris.
>
> (III, 130-31)

A wind rising at the stern accompanies us as we go, and, finally, we glide in at the ancient shores of the Curetes.

But now, knowing the right site, he is beset by disaster:

> postquam altum tenuere rates nec iam amplius ullae
> apparent terrae, caelum undique et undique pontus,
> tum mihi caeruleus supra caput astitit imber
> noctem hiememque ferens, et inhorruit unda tenebris.
>
> (III, 192-95)

After our ships reached the deep, and no longer any lands appear—only sky and sea everywhere—then a dark rain cloud stopped overhead bringing night and storm, and the waves were roughened with darkness.

From now on Aeneas' problem is one of combating the elements in pursuit of an Italy that steadily recedes before him.

Beginning with Celaeno's prophecy, the future predicted in Book III is much more specific, much less auspicious, and much more accurate. The present in which this prophecy is spoken is the grimmest so far. The Trojans have escaped the storm and reached land; now, to their good fortune, or so it seems at first, they come upon unattended apparently ownerless cattle. Calling Jupiter to share in the spoils (*in partem praedamque*, 223) they are about to begin feasting when the Harpies arrive. The feast is ruined in a particularly unattractive way, the Trojans are unable to drive the Harpies off and they are accused (justly) of being the aggressors and threatened with a dire but appropriate punishment. The Trojans have unwittingly broken the rules of hospitality—how ironic the invitation to Jupiter seems now.

As Aeneas tells Helenus later, Celaeno's is the first inauspicious prophecy he has received; it is also the first to predict a specific situation that he will one day have to cope with. It is, however, in one sense, no more accurate than the earlier optimistic ones; for the fates *do* find a way and the table-eating turns out to be something of a joke (VII, 116). But what actually happens before they can wall their city (III, 255) is much worse than what Celaeno foresees. In VII, Aeneas interprets the table-eating not in terms of Celaeno's words but in terms of something Anchises reportedly foretold:

"cum te, nate, fames ignota ad litora uectum
accisis coget dapibus consumere mensas,
tum sperare domos defessus, ibique memento
prima locare manu molirique aggere tecta."

(VII, 124-27)

When, my son, you are carried to unknown shores and hunger forces you to eat your tables after you have eaten your food, then, tired though you are, remember to hope for homes, there to set up your first houses and build a wall.

To this Aeneas responds:

haec erat illa fames, haec nos suprema manebat
exitiis positura modum.

(VII, 128-29)

This was, then, that hunger, this the last trial awaiting us, destined to put an end to our disasters.

The real catastrophe outdoes by far the predicted catastrophe, and the interpretation that Aeneas gives the predicted catastrophe contrasts so sharply with the actuality that it is bitterly ironic. The real *exitium*, the war, is just about to begin; what has happened before is merely a prelude. So the Sibyl suggested in VI (83-94), and so the poet confirms with his invocation in VII (37-44). Instead of the constructive impulses emphasized by Anchises, the world gives itself over to the destructiveness of war.

60

Celaeno's prophecy is, then, partially misleading, partially true. Helenus' prophecy, which comes next, is at once specific, inauspicious, and accurate. It serves two important purposes. It limits the Trojans' goal by making clear that the part of Italy they are sailing to is still very distant, thus extending the second stage of their exile, in which they know their destination but are unable to get there. It also gives the first indication of the third stage in Aeneas' progress, the knowledge that merely arriving in Italy will not, as seemed earlier, put an end to struggle. Helenus is the first to mention the war in Italy, but it is unemphatic:

> illa [the Sibyl] tibi Italiae populos uenturaque bella
> et quo quemque modo fugiasque ferasque laborem
> expediet, . . .
>
> (III, 458-60)

She will set out for you the peoples of Italy and the coming wars, and how you may escape or endure each trial.

By the end of III, prophecy and the present it has predicted have come somewhat into line with each other. Only when the future looks black does prophecy in the *Aeneid* appear to describe it at all accurately. The present arrived at proves to be much as Helenus has described it, except that he omitted the greatest blow of all, the death of Anchises.

-ii-

It is necessary briefly to recapitulate the three previous books to make Aeneas' situation in Book IV comprehensible. When he first appears in Book I, we see him caught up in so terrible a present that his first wish is to have died in the past. His despair fades as he simulates confidence in a Trojan future out of which Trojans may look back on present trials: *forsan et haec olim meminisse iuuabit* (203); he begins to deal with the present as it is, finding out where they are, looking for survivors, and so on. The present becomes, on the surface, more and more favorable as the book progresses. Venus reveals to him that the ships are safe, the other Trojans arrive and are warmly received, and they all settle down to a sumptuous dinner with Dido, who is already almost in love with Aeneas. The present and future now look eminently secure. The two following books show how unacceptable and illusory the security of this present is. In Book II Aeneas is at first oblivious of the future. He cannot see beyond the destruction of the present. (Consequently Hector's appearance means nothing to him.) He begins to put the past behind him when he sees the handiwork of the gods in Troy's downfall, but it is only after his father is convinced by the portent and its confirmation that Aeneas yields reluctantly and partially to the future.

In Book III there is only one aspect of the expedition of which Aeneas takes full charge, and that is city-founding. Anchises makes himself responsible for most other matters. It is Anchises who gives sailing orders from Troy (9); it is Aeneas who immediately upon arrival in Thrace begins to build (16-17). It is Anchises who misinterprets the Trojans' "ancient mother," Aeneas who straightway begins work on the city (132-34). Anchises, again, interprets portents, explains prophecies, gives the orders necessary to escape Charybdis, receives Achaemenides; Aeneas receives the prophecies and instructions, and characteristically, admires the Troy-like settlement in Buthrotum. By the end of III, though Anchises remains in charge of many details, Aeneas has begun, through the prophecies and his attempts to bring them to pass, to understand what the future is about. At Buthrotum he is still nostalgic for Troy but no longer trying to recreate it.

When the narrative returns to the present in Book IV, however, Aeneas appears to have lost his forward momentum. He appears rarely in this book, and when he does he is entirely passive, the object of Dido's initiative. It is Dido who shows Aeneas the town and again and again demands his story, it is Dido who is not moved by appearances and who calls their connection "marriage." When Mercury arrives, he finds Aeneas at last active, founding fortresses (*fundantem arces*, 260)—but what an occupation for the destined founder of what will one day be Rome![2] It is only after Mercury has spoken that Aeneas wakes up as if from a dream and reacts. Suddenly he is the subject (instead of the object) of a verb, the verb *obmutuit* (he became speechless) implying sharp reaction. Suddenly, too, he is eager to be gone, and his mind busies itself with plans for breaking the news to Dido.

Mercury's prophecy keeps to the vague optimism of the early prophecies in III:

si te nulla mouet tantarum gloria rerum
Ascanium surgentem et spes heredis Iuli
respice, cui regnum Italiae Romanaque tellus
debetur.³

(IV, 272-76)

If the glory belonging to such deeds does not move you at all,
consider Ascanius growing up, the hopes of your heir, Iulus,
to whom the kingdom of Italy and the Roman land is owed.

He mentions no difficulties and nothing at all that relates specifically to the immediate future. His message is adapted to the state of mind of his hearer. As in III the prophecies became more specific and less optimistic as Aeneas became stronger in his commitment, so here, to an Aeneas engrossed in the present, Jupiter speaks through Mercury of *gloria* and *spes*. Prophecy in the *Aeneid* is not, then, merely an anonymous statement of what will take place, an inflexible something fixed by fate; it is a statement of the shapes the future may assume, or be given, through the hopes, fears, or designs of the prophet. As an instrument of education, as in the present instance, it will be shaped by the speaker to suit the needs of the recipient.

Aeneas regresses during the interval of oblivion in Carthage. When Dido confronts him with his design for departure, his first wish is to return to Troy, and only the impossibility of that turns him again forward:

me si fata meis paterentur ducere uitam
auspiciis et sponte mea componere curas,
urbem Troianam primum dulcisque meorum
reliquias colerem, Priami tecta alta manerent,
et recidiua manu posuissem Pergama uictis.
sed nunc Italiam magnam Gryneus Apollo,
Italiam Lyciae iussere capessere sortes;
hic amor, haec patria est. . . .

(IV 340ff.)

If my fates allowed me to live my life under my own auspices
and to settle my worries in my own way, I would, first, tend the
city of Troy and sweet remains of my own people, Priam's tall
house would remain, and I would, with my own hands, have
established a renewed Pergamum for the conquered. As it is, it
is great Italy that Grynean Apollo, Italy that the Lycian
prophecies have commanded me to seize. There is my love,
there my country.

His longing for Troy and the past floods his speech with references
to himself: *me, meis auspiciis, sponte mea, meorum reliquias,
colerem, posuissem,* whereas in the three lines devoted to Italy and
the future there is no reference to himself and even the object of the
verb, *iussere,* is left unexpressed. That verb, "ordered," has two
mighty subjects, *Gryneus Apollo* and *Lyciae sortes;* the comple-
mentary infinitive *capessere* has for its object *Italiam* twice, all of
this overpowering the *me* assumed to accompany the infinitive.
Italy is the only *amor,* the only *patria* Aeneas can now have, but his
words show no desire for it; his desire is to rewrite the past.

As the poem continues, it takes Aeneas some time to regain
the fixity and determination he began to acquire in Book III. Book
V, an interlude, allows the Aeneas of Book IV to become the
Aeneas of Book VI by returning to the place and point in his career
where he gave up active control of his destiny, Anchises' death at
Drepanum. The games allow time and scope for Aeneas to assume
the burden of true leadership. At this point, however, he is still not
absolutely committed to the future. His reaction to the ship-
burning is striking both in its resemblance to, but also in its
difference from, his reaction to Mercury in IV:

at pater Aeneas casu concussus acerbo
nunc huc ingentis, nunc illuc pectore curas
mutabat, uersans,

(V, 700-702)

But Father Aeneas, shaken by the bitter event, was turning his
enormous worries over in his mind, shifting them now this
way, now that,

and

> atque animum nunc huc celerem nunc diuidit illuc
> in partisque rapit uarias perque omnia uersat.
>
> > (IV, 285-86, repeated VIII, 20-21)

> Now here, now there, everywhere he divides and hurls his
> swift thoughts; they rove through every possibility.

The lines in IV reflect mental flexibility and swiftness of thought
as Aeneas' mind races over all the possibilities. Those in V reflect
the heaviness and worry of a man overcome by calamity.[4] Aeneas
needs the advice of Nautes and particularly its corroboration by
Anchises before he is capable of moving forward again. This is the
only occasion in the poem when Aeneas is admonished by a
mortal, and his response is again to worry rather than to take
thought and act:

> talibus incensus dictis senioris amici
> tum uero in curas animo diducitur omnis.
>
> > (V, 719-20)

> Aeneas is aroused by such words from his old friend, then
> truly his mind is torn from worry to worry.

It is only after Anchises' appearance that Aeneas again takes the
initiative.

Anchises (724ff.) renews the war theme for the first time since
Helenus' hint in III. A little stronger and more explicit now,

> . . . gens dura atque aspera cultu
> debellanda tibi Latio est,
>
> > (V, 730-31)

> In Latium you must defeat in battle a people hard and
> uncivilized,

its dimensions still remain unapprehended, and it is presented
largely as a justification for leaving the weaker people behind. It is
only in VI, when Aeneas has finally reached Italian soil, that

prophecy and reality begin to coincide. The Sibyl's prophecy
(83ff.) is in some ways an answer to Creusa's. The Trojans have
arrived in Italy, an achievement that was to bring the end of
troubles; here it is suggested that troubles have only just begun.
The Tiber, which Creusa saw flowing gently, now foams with
blood. To replace the kingdom and royal wife promised by
Creusa, we find:

> causa mali tanti coniunx iterum hospita Teucris
> externique iterum thalami.

> (VI, 93-94)

The cause of such evil to the Trojans is, once again, a foreign
wife, once again a foreign marriage.

The future here is painted almost entirely black, but Aeneas is now
ready for it and responds calmly (103-05). And in her last words the
Sibyl does offer a little hope. Her reference to a road to safety *(uia
prima salutis)* leads to the last directional prophecy, the Tiber's in
Book VIII.

Early in Book VIII, the river god assures Aeneas that he has
reached the right spot—*certa, certi, haud incerta* (39, 49) and tells
him not to worry about the war. The degree of revelation is again
suited to Aeneas' situation. Having reached the right place,
Aeneas has begun to worry seriously about the war. He is beset
with worries as in Book V, though now he shows the quickness of
mind in dealing with them that characterized his reaction to
Mercury in IV. At this point Tiber reinterprets the sow portent,
making it less auspicious than it appeared to be in Book III. There
the sow was to signify that Aeneas had reached the right spot:

> cum tibi sollicito secreti ad fluminis undam
> litoreis ingens inuenta sub ilicibus sus
> triginta capitum fetus enixa iacebit,
> alba solo recubans, albi circum ubera nati,
> is locus urbis erit, requies ea certa laborum.

> (III, 389ff.)

When, in your distress, you find, by the water of a hidden
river, lying under the oaks on the shore, a huge sow delivered
of 30 young, a white sow lying on the ground with white

66

offspring around her udders, there will be the place for the city, there certain respite from your labors.

But now, in the situation set up for the sow—when Aeneas is lying in distress by the river—Tiber appears and changes the sow's significance from present respite to future construction.[5] She becomes a sign that Tiber's words are not empty and that Ascanius will found Alba in thirty years (47-48). So once more, in the last of the series of "songes prophétiques"[6] leading Aeneas to the brink of war, as soon as the future becomes present, much of what was good or constructive in it moves ahead to become a new future. There will be no present cessation of troubles for Aeneas.

To sum up: in the directional prophecies as a group, the future appears most hopeful when least apprehended and becomes more specific and more pessimistic only as Aeneas grows in fortitude. The narrative present always seems on the point of attaining the good that is promised, but never quite does. Instead, there is a series of attempted beginnings, each failing and yielding to another. When Aeneas is left on his own after Book VIII with no constructive guidance from the future, the last labor, the last attempt at a new beginning is at hand—a war. This war forces the Trojans to fight the rightful inhabitants of a country (as in the Harpy episode). In fulfilling their destiny they are not allowed to escape the role of aggressor against people who have not harmed them. The neat Vergilian patterning, which places at the beginning of VIII Aeneas' last information about his future, and at the end of it the shield depicting the last major portion of the Augustan future,[7] suggests that the poet expected his Roman readers to see Aeneas' experience in the light of their own, and to perceive their own connections with the distant past. As we shall see as we study the Roman prophecies in detail, Aeneas' future (Augustan present and past) will not be different in kind from Aeneas' present (remote Augustan past).

-*iii*-

As we turn to the Roman prophecies, we must modify our method of examination, since these prophecies are not fulfilled within the poem. They exist outside of the narrative of the poem, outside of

67

time.[8] Thus Aeneas, who gradually learns about the future as he attempts to follow the directions given him, cannot fully understand the Roman prophecies and remains essentially ignorant (*ignarus*, VIII, 730). As Auden put it:

No, Virgil, no:
Not even the first of the Romans can learn
His Roman history in the future tense,
Not even to serve your political turn:
Hindsight as foresight makes no sense.[9]

Not even the first of the Romans can learn his history in the future tense, and Aeneas, who is presented with his history in the future tense, does *not* learn it. But the reader and the poet have a second point of view based on their knowledge of what actually happened historically—what is prophecy to Aeneas is, after all, history to Augustus—and Vergil has encouraged his audience to use this second viewpoint by the device I called the Augustan present and examined in chapter three. Since we can compare predictions with historical realities, the significance of the prophecies to us will be different from their significance to Aeneas. In Book VI, for example, Aeneas watches the procession of historical figures and is told something about each by Anchises. After describing Augustus' achievements, Anchises says:

et dubitamus adhuc uirtutem extendere factis,
aut metus Ausonia prohibet consistere terra?

(VI, 806-7)

And do we hesitate still to expand our valor by deeds, or does fear keep us from occupying the land of Ausonia?

A glimpse of what the future offers may inspire Aeneas to greater efforts in his own present, but, as is to be expected, if the pattern of the directional prophecies holds true for the Roman ones, the Augustan future which is to inspire Aeneas will be much less auspicious when fulfilled than when predicted.

If we examine the three Augustan prophecies in order, we find

68

that they, in fact, seem to insinuate limitations of Rome's potential. Jupiter in Book I speaks very generally, touching on events from Aeneas' war to the binding of Furor; Anchises leaves out all the events of the *Aeneid*, begins with Alba and continues to the death of Marcellus; the shield made by Vulcan begins with Romulus and ends with the victory at Actium. Thus the temporal scope of each is smaller than the last, both at beginning and end. Corresponding to this diminution of temporal scope is a diminution of Rome's power and glory. The prophecy in Book I gives Rome possibilities unlimited,

> his ego nec metas rerum nec tempora pono:
> imperium sine fine dedi,
>
> (I, 278-79)

> For these I set no limits to their fortunes—either of space or of time. I have given them power without end,

emphasizing Augustan peace. The remaining prophecies and the whole narrative of the poem contract these possibilities. Jupiter's prediction is like Creusa's in its lack of specifics, its easy promise of greatness to come. As in hers, arrival in Italy seems to promise an end to toil and an easy future; so in his, Rome's founding seems to lead directly and serenely to the Julians and peace. The later instructional prophecies and the narrative present qualify her view, the later Augustan prophecies and Roman history qualify his.

Anchises' prophecy begins with Aeneas' direct descendants, Silvius and a selection of early Albans. He sums up their achievements with a list of the cities they will found, names which evoke Rome's early struggles in Italy.[10] The first overt suggestion of war comes with Romulus. Romulus is connected with Mars *(Mauortius)*, his attribute the warrior's crest, and war is thus associated with Rome from her very founding. Caesar and his line follow Romulus, after which Anchises dwells on the achievements of Augustus, though only in terms of conquest. This is the brightest part of the whole prophecy, a new Golden Age. It is what everything else is leading up to, the last and best new beginning in Rome's history.

The glory even of this achievement is diminished by its cost. Numa, a man of peace destined to give Rome a second founding based on law, immediately yields to a warrior whose name evokes memories of the destruction of Alba (less than fifty lines after the poem's account of its founding). Already there is a sense of the evanescent quality of men's achievements. Alba may be replaced by something better, but the city which is (in this account) to be Silvius' contribution to Roman history has already run its course by the time of the third Roman king. Following Tullus is Ancus[11] after whom come the Tarquins and Brutus, very closely linked not only because they share a verse, but also because the customary epithet of Tarquin II, proud *(superbus)*, is attached to Brutus.[12] The founding of the Republic should be a very impressive step in Rome's progress (as it is in Livy's account), but this aspect is almost obliterated by another. The *fasces*, emblem of the consul and therefore of the Republic, becomes the weapon with which a father kills his own sons. If the founding of the monarchy is polluted by the murder of brother by brother—Remus is conspicuous in his absence, for reference to auspices brings him forcefully to mind—the founding of the Republic rests on the slaughter of children by their father, and it is on this aspect of its beginnings that Vergil lingers. Brutus acts on behalf of lovely liberty *(pulchra pro libertate)* and out of love of country *(amor patriae)*, but he is unhappy *(infelix)* and motivated by an immeasurable passion for praise *(laudumque immensa cupido)*. The price paid for glory in the *Aeneid* is always high.

Of the next group, the Drusi have no apparently negative overtones, while the Decii bring to mind long battles with the Latins, an indirect comment, perhaps, on the first battle with Latins, about to begin. Torquatus is an ambiguous figure like Brutus. He exemplifies Roman courage, for, as we know from Livy, (VII, 10), he fought the Gauls single-handed; he is also savage with the ax *(saeuus securi)* and the battle ax becomes a murder weapon. Once again a son is killed by a father, and though the father's cause is good, there remains a blemish on it (Livy, VIII, 7). Camillus, who comes next, is perhaps a hero without blemish, though Livy (V, 21ff.) and Plutarch (7, 1) tell of the people's hostility toward him and his excessive vanity, as well as of his achievements. The references to Caesar and Pompey, which follow, carry the implicit irony a stage further, for they are the protagonists of a civil war, father-in-law against son-in-law. Their enmity intimately affects the nation, they turn their strength against her *in uiscera*. It should not surprise us after this that the ensuing names picked out for special mention by Anchises should be the names of conquerors and other "thunderbolts of war."[13] Nor need it surprise us that the long list ends with the death of the young Marcellus. The Golden Age of Augustus culminates in the loss of his chosen successor.

Augustus himself, in the design of this prophecy, is pulled out of his natural position to appear after Romulus. He is linked with Rome's founder, and this implies that his role and Romulus' have something in common. For as Romulus will found Rome, so Augustus will refound it. Romulus will unify the seven hills in one city, Augustus will unify the world in one *imperium*. Augustus is the farthest extension of Romulus. At the present, all still looks well. But after Anchises has gone through Roman history to arrive again at the age which is to justify all that has passed, we understand that the success of the whole enterprise has become somewhat doubtful. Aeneas, who will found Lavinium, will have a successor in Silvius; Silvius, who will found Alba, will be succeeded by the series of Albans mentioned in the early part of the prophecy; Romulus, who will found Rome, will be followed by Numa; but Augustus, who will found the new Rome, will lose his heir. Vergil describes Marcellus' death as a loss to Rome rather than to Augustus, who can (and repeatedly will) choose a new successor, but I wonder whether it is going too far to see a parallel between the unforgettable picture of Aeneas carrying his past on his shoulders and leading his future by the hand as he flees the flames of Troy in Book II and this vision of Rome's "second founder" supporting the weight of the interminable destiny of war that most of this prophecy invokes as his past, and having, after all, no future to lead. In any case, the prophecy that has so often been assumed to proclaim a glorious future ends with death, not with life, and Marcellus' death casts a shadow back over what has gone before. Here, as in our assessment of the passage as a whole, we should remember that Vergil had his choice of all Rome's heroes, legendary and historical; thus his selection and his ordering of them will not have been random.

Some such interpretation of the death of Marcellus as that suggested above may even be indicated by the nature of the Golden Age itself. In Anchises' prophecy Vergil connects Augustus' Golden Age with Saturnus',

Augustus Caesar, diui genus, aurea condet
saecula qui rursus Latio regnata per arua
Saturno quondam,

(VI, 792-94)

Augustus Caesar, son of a god, who will found a golden age again in Latium through the fields once ruled by Saturnus,

and continues with Augustus' conquests. In Book VIII Evander again refers to Saturnus:

aurea quae perhibent illo sub rege fuere
saecula: sic placida populos in pace regebat,
deterior donec paulatim ac decolor aetas
et belli rabies et amor successit habendi.

(VIII, 324ff.)

The age they call golden existed under that king; and so he continued ruling his peoples in quiet peace until, gradually, an inferior and duller age, the madness of war, and desire for possessions took its place.

Like Augustus, Saturnus gathered people together and gave them laws. There followed a Golden Age, of which the chief quality was peace, yet even so, almost of some inner necessity—*deterior donec*—it deteriorated. Once people had been brought together and had amassed possessions, *belli rabies et amor habendi* had followed as a matter of course. Since Augustus has simply done on an immense scale what Saturnus did on a small one, we may begin to wonder whether *his* Golden Age can be lasting—and this point is enforced by the description of Aeneas' shield, with which Book VIII ends. We should keep in mind, as we examine the shield, that it is the last detailed statement of the future in the poem; thus it will provide the context for all that comes after it.

The description begins with Romulus and Remus in a peaceful pastoral setting: two babies and a wolf, man and beast at peace. The situation is rather like the opening of the Pallanteum passage in that violence is in the past or in the distance, the present is quiet. But on the shield, as elsewhere, peace is short-lived; immediately Romulus is grown up and Remus gone, the Sabine women have been carried off and war begins. The first of several wars on the shield, it is here called new (*nouum*), as if Rome's history consisted of little except war, one new war after another— indeed, the subject of the shield was announced as mainly *bella*.[14] The conflict over, there is a brief moment of peacemaking before we are given the conclusion of another war, already fought. Vergil is silent about the details, giving only the circumstances of Mettus' treachery and its hideous consequences. The context is suggested, however, by the remonstrance addressed to Mettus for failing to keep his word (*at tu dictis, Albane, maneres*, 643), which brings to mind the war, the Alban's promise to help, and the result of the whole affair, the destruction of Alba. Looking back to Anchises' prophecy and the Albans of Aeneas' lineage, we remark once again the instability of imperial achievement. Furthermore, if we think of the war Aeneas is about to wage and win, the war that will bring Latins and Trojans together and conclude Aeneas' career, it is evident that any harmony it establishes will be disrupted again; for Romans will again one day be in the situation that the Trojans are in now.

The first part of the shield has dealt with Latium: Rome against the Sabines and Albans. Now more distant neighbors, the Etruscans, are included. Here again the transiency of imperial achievement is hinted at, for Aeneas is, after all, on the point of making an alliance with the Etruscans through their leader Tarchon, whose name is similar enough to Tarquin's to suggest, perhaps, an analogy. In any case, as he is about to ally with the Etruscans, Aeneas receives a shield that shows Romans fighting Etruscans for their liberty. Again Romans will redo what Trojans have done. Now Vergil moves still farther away from Rome to include the Gauls. Gauls appear in a tableau with Manlius, another hero whose career ended in disaster. Vergil is silent about the future of Manlius, but the mention of the Tarpeian rock (from which he was thrown following his conviction on a charge of plotting to establish a monarchy) may be enough to imply his fate.[15]

Finally, after an interlude dealing with religious practices and beliefs, Rome takes the ultimate step in the gradually increasing expansion that began with the Sabine women. Now, with Italy on her side (678), she turns to the east and witnesses the triumph of Augustus and the long procession of conquered peoples. This conquest is the greatest as well as the most recent in Rome's history. There is, however, no mention of the Golden Age promised in VI, no hint of the peace suggested by the chaining of Furor in I.[16] Though the book ends on a note of triumph for Augustus and Rome, it is a triumph that must be contemplated in the light cast by Anchises' prophecy and an awareness of the implications of Book VIII. We have seen Rome's beginnings in Pallanteum's past, the Saturnian Golden Age, the early kings, Evander's arrival, Cacus' maraudings ended by Hercules, the pastoral and idyllic present (hedged around, however, by war), and Roman history from its beginnings as an ever-widening conquest culminating at last in the conquest of the East. But if the battle of Actium is Rome's greatest victory, it too—in this context—may be seen as having a profoundly negative aspect, and from either of two points of view. Jupiter, to be sure, has assured us that Actium is to be the last of the wars, but we have seen how often the present fulfills the future in a less optimistic manner than we might have supposed: what in the poem guarantees that this is not the case with Actium as well? Assume, however, that Actium *is* the last battle, a glorious breakthrough to long years of peace—even on this reading, the *Aeneid* raises a massive qualification by the very nature of what it shows us about Roman character. In an infinitude of peace, what is to become, we may feel impelled to ask, of the only arts the Romans claim (as Anchises predicts)?

> tu regere imperio populos, Romane, memento
> (hae tibi erunt artes), pacique imponere morem,
> parcere subiectis et debellare superbos.[17]
>
> (VI, 851-53)

> Remember, Roman, you are to rule nations with your power—these will be your arts—to impose the habit of peace, spare those who have been defeated and beat down the proud.

Rome grew out of Pallanteum, and Pallanteum had much of value that Rome has lost. We may think of the simple outdoor festival for Hercules, then of the three hundred temples and the proud doorposts (*superbis postibus*, 721-22), or of the gold of Rome, representing luxury, so different from that of the Golden Age, which meant peace. The intuition of loss in the last words used of the shield balances the intuition of Rome's triumph.

-iv-

So far I have emphasized the negative aspects of the prophecies because, taken as a body and in their contexts, they do produce a less than optimistic picture of the future. At the same time, we must not lose sight of the fact that it is to the future that the possibility of hope of some kind belongs. Book VIII, for instance, ambiguous (as we have seen) when examined in terms of the Roman prophecies, emerges in the light of the whole poem as a kind of high point for Rome as well as for Aeneas. Rome appears at the peak of her power on the shield; Aeneas' mission has received an impressive mark of divine approbation in the bestowal of the shield. Moreover, in Book VII the rightness of his claim to a share in Latium has been insisted upon, first by the portents: the bees (69-70) and Lavinia's harmlessly flaming hair (79-80); then by the prophecy of Faunus (96-98), which Latinus is quick to apply to Aeneas:

> hunc illum fatis externa ab sede profectum
> portendi generum paribusque in regna uocari
> auspiciis . . .
>
> (VII, 255-57)

This was the one the fates pointed out, the son-in-law to come from a foreign realm, called to share equally in Latinus' power.

Aeneas is the fated bridegroom and he is also, as Book VIII emphasizes—through the words of Evander (477, 511-13) and the augur (502-3)—the fated chief. Latium's own river wholeheartedly endorses Aeneas' claim to the land, smoothing his path to alliance with the Etruscans. The essential justice of Aeneas' cause is additionally asserted by the character of the opposition, Mezentius, despiser of the gods, whose own people have risen against him. With such an opponent, Aeneas seems almost a force for right, leading out the good to battle with the wicked. Thus when he sets out for war, he has everything apparently on his side.

But now the character of the poem changes. Every reader has been aware of a difference in the last books. There may be no consensus on what it is, or even on where it begins (is it with Book VII, dividing the poem into Odyssean and Iliadic halves? or with Book IX, dividing it into thirds?[18]), but there is general agreement that something happens to the poem toward its end.[19]

If we examine the last four books as a group, we find that they share a number of distinguishing characteristics (among them a marked increase in the number of similes and direct addresses). Of these distinguishing features only one is related to the question of time and this is the relative disappearance of the prophetic future. The first eight books contain twenty-five directly and indirectly reported prophecies (including portents, which, when interpreted, act as prophecies);[20] the last four books contain four.[21] Thus there are, on the average, three per book in the first part, one per book in the last. (Even if we exclude from our calculations Book III, whose seven prophecies make up a significant proportion of the total, we find an average of over two and one-half prophecies per book in the first group, still a notably larger proportion.) The number of lines devoted to prophecy in Books I-VIII is 513, or slightly over 8 percent of the total lines (6,297); the number of lines in Books IX-XII is 23, less than 1 percent of the total (3,582).[22] It is thus clear at a glance that the future, at least in the shape of prophecy, is far less at issue toward the close of the poem than it was earlier.

Furthermore, of the four prophecies found in the last books, only two, Jupiter's in X and XII, have any real claim on that title. Apollo's to Ascanius (IX, 641-44) barely deserves the name.[23] Unlike other prophecies it is only nominally addressed to a hearer; Ascanius certainly does not hear it. Moreover, it does not predict a specific event but only a general situation, and it has no effect on the course of events. Whatever significance it has takes place in the mind of the reader, a characteristic it shares, as we shall shortly see, with Jupiter's predictions.

Cymodocea's prediction in Book X,

surge age et Aurora socios ueniente uocari
primus in arma iube, et clipeum cape quem dedit ipse
inuictum ignipotens atque oras ambiit auro.
crastina lux, mea si non inrita dicta putaris,
igentis Rutulae spectabit caedis aceruos,

(X, 241-45)

Rise up and, when dawn comes, be quick to have your friends called to arms. Take the invincible shield which the fire-powerful god himself gave you, surrounding its edges with gold. Tomorrow's light, unless you think my words empty, will look upon huge heaps of Rutulian dead,

the very last information about the future that Aeneas is given in the poem, may be compared with Venus' in Book I (390-92), the very first.[24] Both are relatively trivial as prophecy, both predict something that is shortly to be self-evident—Aeneas will find his ships safely returned as soon as he gets to Carthage, and tomorrow he will succeed in battle if he hurries to the Trojan camp. Neither prophecy motivates any new action on the hero's part; both merely confirm him in his present course.

The two prophecies spoken by Jupiter remain to be examined. They are unlike the directional prophecies we looked at above in that they are not addressed to mortals to direct them; and they are unlike the Roman prophecies in that they do not outline Rome's history. Their main design seems to be to create a proper attitude in the reader's mind, contrasting the narrative present as it *is* with the way it *should be*, in terms of Rome's future. The first predicts the Punic Wars:

adueniet iustum pugnae (ne arcessite) tempus,
cum fera Karthago Romanis arcibus olim
exitium magnum atque Alpis immittet apertas:
tum certare odiis, tum res rapuisse licebit.
nunc sinite et placitum laeti componite foedus.

(X, 11-15)

A proper time for war will come one day, do not hurry it, when fierce Carthage will hurl great destruction and the opened Alps at Rome's hills; then will be the time to vie in hatred and to plunder. Now let be and joyfully make the peace I have decided upon.

The second predicts the peaceful coming together of Trojans and Latins:

sermonem Ausonii patrium moresque tenebunt,
utque est nomen erit; commixti corpore tantum
subsident Teucri. morem ritusque sacrorum
adiciam faciamque omnis uno ore Latinos.
hinc genus Ausonio mixtum quod sanguine surget,
supra homines, supra ire deos pietate uidebis,
nec gens ulla tuos aeque celebrabit honores.

(XII, 834-40)

The Ausonians will keep their native language and customs and their name will be as it is. The Trojans will settle in with them, joined in body only. I shall add customs and religious rites, making them all Latins—of one tongue. The race that rises from this with mingled Ausonian blood, you will see surpass men and gods in piety, and no race shall honor you as they do.

Although the predictions differ in content, they both comment sharply on the present. In the first, Jupiter condemns the war outright, using as his contrast the series of wars that had, historically, left an indelible mark on the mind of every Roman. From Rome's long history of wars he could not have chosen a more convincing example of a "right" war to adduce in judgment against the present contest. The Punic wars had been unambiguously fought against a foreign enemy; Aeneas' war, though ambiguous, must be regarded as a civil war, the first of a long line of such in Rome's history. Furthermore, the particular Punic war cited had involved an all-out attack on the Italian homeland by a great military power—*exitium magnum atque Alpis immittet apertas;* Aeneas' war is an affair of a small band of exiles looking

78

for a home. Most important of all, of course, the Punic wars have divine sanction, whereas Aeneas' war contradicts Jupiter's will. No more need be said. Jupiter gives us the measure of all that has been happening and will happen. The fighting that has taken place so far, bringing the loss in particular of Nisus and Euryalus, the fighting that will shortly result in the deaths of Pallas and Lausus: all this is not only unnecessary and foolish, it is also against the will of the father of gods and king of men.

The colloquy with Juno takes place in Book XII when the poem is almost at an end. Its prediction of peace and harmony for the future contrasts sharply with the destruction of the present. The war that has dominated the narrative present for four books, destroying, one after another, so many young warriors (and shortly to take Turnus) is about to end in the desired coalition of Trojan and Latin. Once again, and for the last time, a "wrong" present will be superseded by a "right" future. But reconciliation remains in the future while the narrative present plays itself out in a final blaze of hostility; furthermore, the disparity between the final actions of the poem and their predicted result points up the aimlessness and futility of all the fighting. Other wars in the *Aeneid* end with the subjugation of the conquered, with the triumph and spoils of the conqueror. The scene at the end of Book II when Troy has fallen comes immediately to mind, and the less harsh, but nevertheless similar, scene on Aeneas' shield in Book VIII, contrasting the triumph of Augustus with the procession of captives after Actium. Here, on the contrary, Jupiter promises only the same coalition that Latinus offered earlier, in Book VII, before war broke out. The results of war, in other words, are to be little more than what might have accrued from peaceful acceptance of the stranger. We do not, of course, desire or expect that Aeneas' war will end in Trojan dominion. We may, however, find ourselves again impelled to reflect on the cost at which the Trojan-Roman line seems destined to win its victories. Here, at the very end of the poem, when nothing remains but for Turnus to be killed, Juno makes her requests for the future. Why should war have been necessary to bring this about? Why could not her requests have been made and accepted much earlier?—since a coalition of this sort was always intended. Finally, pondering these questions, relieved to find future harmony (at least) assured—as Juno, whose wrath began Aeneas' troubles (I, 11), leaves the scene reconciled and happy—we are presented with our last glimpse of the narrative present, a chilling sequence.[25] Jupiter summons the fury, Aeneas kills Turnus, and the scene of rage and savagery seems at once an *exemplum* of what is wrong with, and a fitting end to, the narrative present.

In conclusion, then, the almost complete absence of the future in the last four books is a striking fact about them; as is the fact that such prophetic future as is presented is different in the ways I have noted from both sorts of prophecy familiar from the first eight books. There the future served as a backdrop against which the present could be seen and measured, and it also had a more active function—there, the future, like a giant magnet, drew men and issues onward. Here the future no longer offers guidance to the present, drawing Aeneas and Troy along their destined path, it merely comments, generally unfavorably, upon the present, setting off what *is* by glimpses of what *will be*.

Prophecy is, of course, not the only means at Vergil's disposal for referring to the future. Very rarely he reports what will happen in the future tense, as at IX, 446ff. Occasionally he refers to the Augustan present (discussed in chapter three), which is future from the point of view of the narrative, as at XII, 134-35. For the most part, however, Vergil limits his focus to the war between Latins and Trojans and we are left to concentrate on the character of the narrative present.

-*v*-

A striking feature of the present in the last books is its relation to the past.[26] In fact, the past seems to replace the future as counterpoise to the present. Glimpses into the past are usually of the Trojan War and Vergil rewrites the *Iliad* changing the outcome, confusing and conflating the roles. Thus Aeneas is the reluctant Hector to Turnus' fiery Achilles, but he is also, *mutatis mutandis*, the relatively unencumbered invader Achilles to Turnus' city- and family-bound Hector, and he is further, as Turnus points out, the treacherous Paris to Turnus' Menelaus. These shifts in role and character give extra depth and perspective to the events of the present. For our sense of Aeneas here is not complete unless we see that circumstances have forced him into the role of a second Paris as well as into his other roles. It is unfair to Vergil's talent for significant allusion to ignore the implications inherent in such connections, just as it is to assume, with Conington, that the epithet, *Laomedonteus*, at VIII, 18 has no implications.[27]

A second and very obvious aspect of the present in these books is its confusion and disorder, its loss of purpose, resulting from the disappearance of guidance from those who can see the future. Even the divine plan seems, often, not merely to be forgotten, but to have collapsed. In the first eight books, it was clear, through prophecy, that Jupiter had a grand masterplan, containing (at least in outline) everything from the present to the distant future. Nothing, not even the tinkerings of Juno and Venus, could fundamentally disrupt this plan. When the situation began to get out of hand, as in Book IV, Jupiter intervened to correct it. Let us look now at the council of the gods in Book X where Jupiter must deal with divine discord. Though he opens the council with a demand for concord, Venus and Juno have only to complain that harmony is impossible for Jupiter to give in. It is a moment of supreme anticlimax: the two goddesses have made their claims, the king of the gods must rule; four lines expatiate upon his great powers and upon the expectant hush as he prepares to speak:

> tum pater omnipotens, rerum cui prima potestas,
> infit (eo dicente deum domus alta silescit
> et tremefacta solo tellus, silet arduus aether,
> tum Zephyri posuere, premit placida aequora pontus).
> (X, 100-103)

> Then the all-powerful father, whose power is first over all things, begins, and as he speaks, the tall house of the gods grows quiet, earth is shaken at its foundation, the lofty sky is still; then the breezes are laid to rest and the sea presses its waters into calmness.

After proclaiming his intention to make the decision, he states that he will provide no leadership after all—the fates will find a way, *fata uiam inuenient*.[28] When the god whose powers and prerogatives exceed all others' yields to discord because the alliance he intended is not permitted (*haud licitum*) by two lesser divinities, we can hardly expect mere mortals to take a stand against discord.

81

Later in the same book, moreover, we find Jupiter not merely yielding to an existing state of disharmony but actually contributing to it. At 606ff. he incites Juno to take a hand in the war (the voluntary nature of his move emphasized by the word *ultro*). It is at his instigation that Mezentius joins battle, setting off the sequence of events that culminates in Lausus' death—all this in a book that began with the royal command to make peace—*nunc sinite et placitum laeti componite foedus*. This is surely a very different sort of involvement in human affairs from his sending of Mercury to ensure that Rome will come to be.

Things are no better on the human level. Each book presents some new aspect of the lack of coherence and direction, the folly and futility, the disregard of the future, that warfare entails. Book IX shows confusion from beginning to end. Aeneas' absence, a piece of extraordinary good fortune for the Italians (as Iris points out)—*quod optanti diuum promittere nemo / auderet*, 6-7—does them no good, the attempt to fire the ships fails and Turnus almost consciously misinterprets its significance. Guards are stationed and proceed to drink themselves into a stupor, *somno uinoque soluti* (the phrase echoing that used to describe Troy buried in sleep and wine, *somno uinoque sepultam*, II, 265, on her last night, the Italians' arrogance now pointed up by the Trojans' tragic error then). The Trojans succeed no better. The heroism of Nisus and Euryalus is disastrously canceled out by their mad slaughter, as Nisus realizes too late. When Pandarus and Bitias open the gate they offer Turnus an unparalleled opportunity, as the poet carefully notes (757-59). If we think all this merely emphasizes the Trojans' dependence on Aeneas,[29] we should expect Aeneas' return to restore order at least to the Trojan side. But Book X offers instead not only Jupiter's condemnation of the war, but also disintegrations within Aeneas himself as he loses his self-control after Pallas' death (witness the hostages destined to be immolated on Pallas' pyre, the slaughter of a suppliant, the "sacrifice" of a priest, and finally the killing of Lausus.[30] Are these actions that the new Troy will honor?) Book XI is devoted almost entirely to exhibiting the idiocies of war—in the magnificent speech of Drances, in Aeneas' failure to await the verdict on his peace proposals before renewing the attack, in the pathetically gratuitous death of Camilla, in the abortive ambush that Turnus rashly leaves moments before Aeneas rides safely through.[31] To this series of disconnected events, Book XII adds the ultimate humiliation of the principals, not least of Aeneas who endangers his whole enterprise when he forgets his bride, and with her, the claims of the future—that long line of descendants to result from their union—in his desire to destroy:

> urbem hodie, causam belli, regna ipsa Latini,
> ni frenum accipere et uicti parere fatentur,
> eruam et aequa solo fumantia culmina ponam.
>
> (XII, 567-69)

> Unless they accept the bit in defeat and agree to obey us, today
> I shall raze their city, the cause of the war, Latinus' own
> kingdom, and level its smoking heights with the ground.

Amata commits suicide, Latinus is crushed by sorrow and guilt, Turnus is killed, and Lavinia is left, spoils for a victor whose victory in some way demeans him.

All in all, in these last books, Vergil creates not merely a fitting conclusion to the narrative present, but also a melancholy commentary on the war-filled future that is to be Rome's glory but also her bane. We know that this war is, in fact, the last obstacle Aeneas must confront in order to give Rome birth, but it is easy to forget that it has a purpose, since even Aeneas forgets at moments, and it is in any case natural to wonder to what extent ends can ever justify means. The first books of the poem have shown us Roman history as largely a series of wars. The last ones, as if to intensify our hesitations about means, give a close look at war that is not a pretty one. On the shield Vergil presented Rome's history as little but war, there schematized and distanced, made into a work of art. The figures, whether legendary or historical, were removed from time—they were only likenesses: *illum indignanti similem similemque minanti / aspiceres*, 649-50 (like one angered, like one threatening), frozen forever in their various postures (like the lovers on Keats' Grecian urn). In the books that follow, Vergil paints a "real" war in words, and by his treatment of it, seems to suggest that war breeds its own madness, a madness that refuses to look beyond the needs of the present.

It is entirely in keeping with the character of these last books that the *Aeneid* just stops at Turnus' death—there is no conclusion, no drawing up of loose threads, no look, however brief, at what has been achieved, what is likely to follow. From Jupiter's prophecy in Book I we know what is to follow:

> . . . moresque uiris et moenia ponet,
> tertia dum Latio regnantem uiderit aestas
> ternaque transierint Rutulis hiberna subactis.
>
> (I, 264-266)

He shall establish customs and walls for men when the third summer has seen him ruling in Latium and three winters have passed since the Rutulians' defeat.

How simple it all sounds! But one thing that Aeneas' career should have taught us is that it certainly will not be simple or unambiguous.

By neglecting the future in these books Vergil manages, in fact, to imply a great deal about it. He has given us the terms in which to look at the present in the first eight books in the alternation between predicted future and its realization in the present; in the last books he submerges his characters in the present and allows his readers to draw what lessons they will.

V

CONCLUSION

It is clear to most of us who study the *Aeneid* today that those of
our predecessors who read it as a poor copy of Homeric epic, and
those who read it as an unqualified glorification of Augustus' rule,
were missing something important; we may assume, however,
that future readers will marvel at the blindspots in our readings.[1]
Vergil's habit of continually reexamining and redefining things
makes his poetry elusive. The *Aeneid* presents Rome as a jewel of
many facets, some of them spectacularly bright and shining, as
past readers saw clearly, many of them dimmed and dull, as
modern readers have emphasized. So rich and varied is the pattern
that we can never rest with the conviction that we have finally
figured it all out, grasped what is there to grasp, any more than
Aeneas is ever allowed actually to catch hold of those things which
he continually reaches out for. Nevertheless, it is time now to reach
out for something, to try to draw some conclusions about the
Aeneid and time.

I observed earlier that writers of epic before Vergil were not
very interested in the question of time. Greek epic is largely
concerned with the dramatic present—past and future providing
the barest framework for present events. The *Aeneid* gives the
present enormous visual and psychological impact, owing to
Vergil's manipulations of tense. At the same time, however, it
could be said to be concerned with the future—the *results* of the
action in the present—as much as with the present itself. Vergil
involved his listeners in a new way in the experience of a poem
when he confronted them with their own present and recent
bloody past predicted as the culmination of a great task in the
narrative present, and so gave his subject great immediacy and

enormous historical significance. We have many works in English that play with the notion of time in various ways (*Berkeley Square*,[2] for example, or *Orlando*,[3] or much of science fiction). Is there any that so involves the reader in the events it depicts that he could hardly forget in reading it that his historical or "real" present has its ancestry in, and depends on the successful completion of, long past events? I can think of none.

Even when the reader of the *Aeneid* is disengaged from Aeneas' present by the second (or, what I have called Augustan) present tense, he is still concerned with Rome and the Roman world, now merely from a different point of view. The effect is like the "solecism of the two presents" experienced by a reader of novels who

> is jerked from the battlefield of long ago where he was witnessing or performing superhuman feats of valour back to the armchair before the fire with a ripe November fog pressing against his windows. . . . The sense of immediateness and presentness, which the reader enjoys on the plane of "fictional" time is destroyed by the implied reference to his chronological time, his moment of present sensation.[4]

The effect is also slightly different from that; for the reader of the *Aeneid* is jolted from the fictional world to an awareness of the real world, but it is from his contemplation of one long distant world to the world it helped create. The two presents are, accordingly, not mutually exclusive, like the battlefield and the November fog, they are causally intertwined, each helping to define the other. Thus one effect of Vergil's management of time is to make his reader accept the narrative present, some 1,000 years past, as bound up in his own present. A second and related effect is to make the *Aeneid* a peculiarly Roman poem. We feel that Rome is its real subject, from the opening sentence, which ends with the establishment of her lofty walls (*altae moenia Romae*, I, 7), to the very last, when Turnus' death clears away the last obstacle to Lavinium's establishment, thus opening the way to Rome. If we subtract Achilles from the *Iliad* or Odysseus from the *Odyssey*, there is no story to tell; if we take away Aeneas, the first Roman, from the *Aeneid*, there is no Rome to provide either poet or audience, so inextricably is historical Rome linked to her legendary founder.

Conclusion

The *Aeneid* seems, then, a very Roman poem, rooted in the historical realities of a now long-gone civilization; yet, it has seemed to many to be in some way universal—certainly past readers like Dante must have thought so—and Aeneas has been thought of as representing Everyman. Its special use of time contributes greatly to our sense that the *Aeneid* (like the *Georgics*) has something to say to us now. By his manipulations of tense and time, Vergil seems to abolish time, creating a sort of "timeless now," which belongs as much to us in the twentieth century as it did to Dante in the fourteenth or Augustus long before that. Thus what the *Aeneid* has to say about Rome is about all civilization, and what it has to say about Aeneas is about the human condition—the *Aeneid*, rooted in time, becomes itself timeless, for all time. It involves all its readers in Rome's destiny; it makes us all Romans.

A further result of Vergil's conflation of times is a profound sense of loss; for what Rome has become is juxtaposed with all she might have been. When Book VIII, for example, shows her beginnings in Pallanteum (and, even further back, in the Golden Age of Saturnus), it is a portrait of progress, of course, but it also communicates a sense of loss. We are all aware of loss as an inevitable part of human life and of progress—opportunities lost, paths not taken—but, gradually, as time goes by, we tend to forget what was, or might have been. Vergil does not let us forget—not in the *Eclogues*, with its oppositions of bucolic leisure and civic turmoil; not in the *Georgics*, with its apparent idealization of country life, which does not, however, forget the birds, who lose their ancestral homes to the farmer's plough (II, 209-10); and certainly not in the *Aeneid*, where Vergil keeps Aeneas' present and future, Augustus' past and present (the same span of time looked at from different points of view) constantly before us.

It is time that allows redefinition and revision, time that reveals the hidden pattern of things. ("Time teaches all, as it grows old,"[5] says Prometheus in Aeschylus' play.) The pattern that time reveals in the *Aeneid* is essentially pessimistic. Late Republican and Augustan writers tend to look back fondly on the past, but the view of time and history suggested in the *Aeneid* cannot be defined as merely nostalgic. By his grouping of heroes in the panorama in Book VI, Vergil suggests that a hard look at the grand old men of the Republic will cast some doubts on the putative perfections of the "good old days." But the *Aeneid* also throws grave doubts on the possibilities for progress. Can we really conclude that Augustan peace justifies all that has happened, wiping out (as in the 4th *Eclogue*) all the failures of the past?

How far, finally, has Rome progressed from her beginnings by the end of the *Aeneid*? (How far has the process of civilization itself progressed?) At times Rome is made to seem something totally new, the end product of an enormous temporal and spatial, even moral, convergence. At other moments, she seems to be not different in kind, only different in scale, from all that went before—just as her wars may be seen as little more than a redoing, on an ever-increasing scale, of Aeneas' Italian war. (Similarly, Aeneas himself seems at times a being quite different from, and more highly civilized than, his associates, uniquely suited to the great and difficult destiny that is his; at other moments, however, as in Books X and XII, it seems that civilization is merely a veneer, which falls off under stress, revealing a savagery and inhumanity alien to less civilized men like Turnus.[6]) Often we feel impelled to conclude that there is no substantive change, that when things look good, it is either because they have not been examined, or because they are too distant to see properly. Thus the prophecies, read with an eye to what actually happens, seem less optimistic than at first hearing—when time and the close-up view have shown us their other side, they lose some of their lustre. And so it is with much of the poem. The process of definition and redefinition that goes on in the *Aeneid* has, by the end, cast shadows on past, present, and future. Troy failed, as Aeneas was forced to acknowledge when he saw the gods tearing the city down; Aeneas' present toils are merely obstacles in the path of a better future; but what is good in the future seems repeatedly to elude its pursuer's grasp. Desire, struggle, and loss—this is the *Aeneid*, where people, like the dead in Book VI, reach out in longing for things they cannot capture:

tendebantque manus ripae ulterioris amore.

(VI, 314)

And they held out their arms in longing for the further bank.

Appendix I
Zeugma and Hendiadys

Two verbal peculiarities, which are notable in the *Aeneid* and deserve further study, are the tropes zeugma and hendiadys. They seem to reflect and shed light on the Vergilian habit of mind underlying the phenomenon that has been my major theme, his patterns of time. Though these tropes are found in other Latin poets, Vergil's use of them strikes me as characteristically his own.

We must first, of course, establish what is meant by hendiadys and zeugma. Hendiadys is defined nowadays as a "figure of speech in which a single idea is expressed by two words connected by a conjunction, e.g., by two substantives with *and* instead of an adjective and a substantive"; and zeugma as "a figure by which a single word is made to refer to two or more words in the sentence; especially when applying in sense to only one of them, or applying to them in different senses" *(OED)*. These definitions, intended to describe English tropes, will serve for their ancient counterparts as well.[1]

What is the effect of such tropes? The commentators do not much help us, pointing to their repeated occurrence but failing to indicate what we are to make of it. Conington, for example, on *Aeneid* II, 116, one of Vergil's most notable instances of hendiadys: *sanguine placastis uentos et uirgine caesa* (you appeased the winds by means of blood and a young girl slain), says simply, "hendiadys, which is expressed v. 118 by two clauses"; and Page, on I, 293-94;

> . . . dirae ferro et compagibus artis
> claudentur Belli portae . . .

once he has translated the hendiadys ("the gates of war grim with

89

iron and close-fastened bars"), has nothing to add except, "Hendiadys - 'close-fastened bars of iron.'" By labeling and thus apparently disposing of the expression, both commentators encourage us to dismiss it rather than to ask questions about its poetic role.[2]

What do we discover if we do ask questions, if we try to find out what the Conington example means? Would we make discoveries? I think we might. The phrase occurs when the oracle (in Sinon's fictional account) advises the Greeks who are eager to go home but are prevented by storms:

"sanguine placastis uentos et uirgine caesa,
cum primum Iliacas, Danai, uenistis ad oras;
sanguine quaerendi reditus animaque litandum
Argolica."

(II, 116-19)

You appeased the winds by blood and a young girl slain, Greeks, when first you came to Ilian shores. By blood your return must by sought, propitiation must be made with a Greek life. . . .

Hendiadys here may be said to make a single idea out of two words, as its name suggests, but it might be more accurate to describe its effect as making two ideas out of one by presenting its two aspects separately. Vergil's phrase, *sanguine . . . et uirgine caesa*, expresses two notions—"blood" and "slaughtered girl," the equivalent "ordinary" expression, *sanguine uirginis caesae* (by the blood of a slaughtered girl), only one—"blood." In the ordinary expression *uirginis* merely specifies the blood's owner; it has no direct connection with *placastis* on which the ablative depends. In the hendiadys, on the other hand, the girl receives equal weight with the blood, and the separation of the blood from the girl makes Vergil's statement surprising, and, in my opinion, grimmer than the normal locution would be. At the very least, the grammatical disjunction of the blood from its source calls attention to itself, extends the area of discourse, and insists on being "interpreted." Other examples are less dramatic, perhaps, than the above—*palmam Entello taurumque relinquunt*, V, 472 (they leave the

90

prize and the bull to Entellus), for example, or, *Ilioneus saxo atque ingenti fragmine montis* . . . *sternit,* IX, 569-71 (Ilioneus flattens [Lucetius] with a rock and an enormous fragment of a mountain)—but, like it, they suggestively expand into two notions what might only have expressed one. Since the unexpected has more impact than the expected, it is a device that a poet can use to help us look with his eyes and perceive more than we ordinarily do.

Even more economical, and perhaps more typically Vergilian than hendiadys, is zeugma. Zeugma makes one word, commonly a verb, suffice where two might have seemed necessary, compressing two ideas into one, joining elements that are, strictly speaking unjoinable. It is, thus, the polar opposite to hendiadys—the other side of the coin. Book X, 692, offers a good example: *uni odiisque uiro telisque frequentibus instant* (they pursue a single man with crowds of hatreds and weapons). Here *odia,* an abstract noun, is not strictly suitable with *instant,* or, in any event, *tela* is more obviously appropriate. Yet *odia,* treated zeugmatically as the exact equivalent of *telis,* takes on some of the overtones of the concrete noun and thus becomes itself a weapon. It is both the reason for the weapons and one of them. Zeugma, then, facilitates the telescoping of unlikes. Here, for example, the cause is made part of the act. Elsewhere,—e.g.,

> inclusos utero Danaos et pinea furtim
> laxat claustra Sinon,
>
> (II, 258-59)

> Secretly Sinon looses the Greeks closed up in the belly [of the wooden horse] and the pine bolts,

the *consequence* of an action is made part of its inception. Sinon looses the bolts and thereby frees the Greeks, but in the zeugmatic form the Greeks become as much the objects of Sinon's manipulation as the bolts he actually shifts. We are encouraged to look twice and reflect on what is literally being said.

The link-word in zeugma need not be a verb. It can be a preposition:

. . . quae moenia clausis
ferrum acuant portis in me excidiumque meorum.

(VIII, 385-86)

what towns with closed gates sharpen steel for me and the
destruction of my people.

The sense of the preposition varies with its object—*against* me, *for
the purpose of* destruction. In the expression *horridus in iaculis et
pelle Libystidis ursae*, V, 37 (bristling in javelins and the skin of a
Libyan bear), there is no verb; the adjective *horridus* is the
zeugmatic link—two different sorts of bristling become one. In
each case there is a certain oddness, a certain unexpectedness, of
expression, which, allusive and often untranslatable, suggests
much more than its nonzeugmatic equivalent.

Similar to zeugma, but strictly speaking not zeugmatic
because there is no link of the sort we have been examining, are
such collocations of words as that found at *Aeneid* I, 421-22:

miratur molem Aeneas, magalia quondam,
miratur portas strepitumque et strata uiarum.[3]

Aeneas marvels at the massive buildings, formerly huts, he
marvels at the gates, the noise and the paved streets.

Here, masses, objects, and noises are all treated as if they were the
same kind of thing. Some particularly striking examples are those
that link abstract nouns with concrete, as at IX, 598: *non pudet
obsidione iterum ualloque teneri* (are you not ashamed to be held
once again in siege and rampart) or VIII, 226-27: *saxum, ferro
quod et arte paterna / pendebat* (a rock which was hanging by
means of iron and a father's skill)—*teneri* or *pendebat* goes
naturally enough with either noun by itself; in each case, the
joining of the two is noteworthy. In the latter, both the material
used and the inventiveness that devised the hinge are means, but
means of very different sorts, here made to appear as two aspects of
the same thing. So again, at II, 250-52:

uertitur interea caelum et ruit Oceano nox
inuoluens umbra magna terramque polumque
Myrmidonumque dolos . . .

Meanwhile the sky turns and night rushes down to the ocean,[4]
wrapping in great shadow land and heaven and the tricks of
the Greeks.

Here, *inuoluens* could easily be applied metaphorically to *dolos;*
what is memorable is the association of trickery with land and
sky.[5]

We may now begin to see how hendiadys and zeugma, in a
sense opposites, can be very similar in their rhetorical reach. It is,
in fact, often very difficult to decide which term is suitable. At III,
414, for example—*haec loca ui quondam et uasta conuulsa ruina*
(these places were once torn loose by force and a vast overthrow)—
is the juxtaposition of *ui* and *uasta ruina* to be called zeugma or
hendiadys? Furthermore, what are we to term the famous example
in Book X:

adueniet iustum pugnae (ne arcessite) tempus,
cum fera Karthago Romanis arcibus olim
exitium magnum atque Alpis immittet apertas.

(X, 11-13)

A proper time for war will come one day, do not hurry it,
when fierce Carthage will hurl great destruction and the
opened Alps at Rome's hills.

The commentators, though hesitant, agree in calling it
hendiadys. Page states that it may be taken "as a sort of
hendiadys" (although he prefers to take it "with rhetorical
boldness" as the Alps themselves "let loose on Rome because
they let the invaders through their passes").[6] Conington
claims that it "almost forms a hendiadys." What is clear,
however, is that it could equally well be called zeugma,
linking two objects of different orders, as in the earlier very
impressive example at I, 68: *Ilium in Italiam portans uictos-
que penatis* (bringing to Italy Troy and conquered household

gods).[7] Hendiadys and zeugma may be said, then, to be merely two aspects of the same tendency—to see connections in diversity, multiplicity in unity. If we are alert to these nuances in Vergil's style, we are more likely to be alert to larger issues in his poetry. For the habit of mind—the tendency to synthesize, to expand the possibilities of language by juxtaposition—that produced these tropes is so basic to Vergil's art that it reaches out beyond matters of style, becoming an important ordering principle for his poetry in its wider aspects.

APPENDIX II

TENSES IN OVID AND LUCAN

I studied two substantial passages from Ovid and two from Lucan
to try to determine whether Vergil's use of tenses was, in fact,
noteworthy, or whether it was standard epic practice. The
passages were chosen at random in the sense that I selected them
before examining them and so I had no idea what I would find
when I began to count tenses. I did, however, try to find narrative
passages that seemed to have something in common with the
narrative of the *Aeneid,* passages which described action in process
and which were not continually interrupted by direct speech. The
statistics proved to be interesting and I hope to make a further
study of the material in the future. At this stage, I do not hope to
say anything which will shed new light on either Ovid or Lucan. I
only want to point out that my preliminary study of these two
poets suggests that their handling of tenses is rather different from
Vergil's. I am not sure that I have discovered the principles on
which either of my "control" poets operates, and I am well aware
that a mere handful of verses makes a shaky foundation for any
sort of theory, but, it does seem that, at the very least, Ovid and
Lucan construct their scenes with a different pattern of tenses from
that which we have observed in Vergil, or, perhaps, with no
pattern at all. I shall look first at the two passages from Ovid, then
at the two from Lucan.

. . . dixit dextraque molarem
sustulit et magnum magno conamine misit.   60
illius inpulsu cum turribus ardua celsis
moenia mota forent, serpens sine vulnere mansit
loricaeque modo squamis defensus et atrae

duritia pellis validos cute reppulit ictus;
65 at non duritia iaculum quoque vicit eadem:
quod medio lentae spinae curvamine fixum
constitit, et totum descendit in ilia ferrum.
    ille dolore ferox caput in sua terga retorsit
vulneraque adspexit fixumque hastile momordit,
70 idque ubi vi multa partem labefecit in omnem,
vix tergo eripuit; ferrum tamen ossibus haesit.
tum vero postquam solitas accessit ad iras
causa recens, plenis tumuerunt guttura venis,
spumaque pestiferos circumfluit albida rictus,
75 terraque rasa sonat squamis, quique halitus exit
ore niger Stygio, vitiatas inficit auras.
ipse modo inmensum spiris facientibus orbem
cingitur, interdum longa trabe rectior adstat,
inpete nunc vasto ceu concitus imbribus amnis
80 fertur et obstantes proturbat pectore silvas.
    cedit Agenorides paullum spolioque leonis
sustinet incursus instantiaque ora retardat
cuspide praetenta: furit ille et inania duro
vulnera dat ferro figitque in acumine dentes.
85 iamque venenifero sanguis manare palato
coeperat et virides adspergine tinxerat herbas;
sed leve vulnus erat, quia se retrahebat ab ictu
laesaque colla dabat retro plagamque sedere
cedendo arcebat nec longius ire sinebat,
90 donec Agenorides coniectum in gutture ferrum
usque sequens pressit, dum retro quercus eunti
obstitit et fixa est pariter cum robore cervix.
pondere serpentis curvata est arbor et ima
parte flagellari gemuit sua robora caudae.

                                    (*Metamorphoses* III, 59-94)

He spoke, and with his right hand lifted a great boulder, and
threw it with a tremendous effort. By the shock high walls
with their lofty towers would have been shaken, but the
serpent remained unwounded. Protected by his scales and his
dark, unyielding hide as by a breastplate, he repelled the
strong blows with his skin. But the same inflexibility did not

overcome the spear—which stopped, impaled in the central coil of his tough back, and sank its whole iron length in his flank. Wild with pain he twisted his head around to his back, and looked at the wound, and bit at the shaft of the implanted spear. And after he worked it loose with great violence, he wrenched it—with difficulty—from his back, but the iron head stuck in the bone. Then indeed fresh cause intensified his normal wrath, his throat swelled with full veins, white foam slavering his pestilential jaws, and the land echoes with the scraping of his scales, and a stench like the black breath from the opening to Styx fouls the breezes. Now he coils himself into a huge ball, now he stretches out taller than a tall tree, now he is borne along with an irresistible rush, like a river aroused by storms, and he flattens with his breast the obstructing forests. Cadmus, son of Agenor, yields a little and receives the onrush on his lion skin and turns back the grasping jaws with extended spear. The serpent rages and gives wounds in vain to the hard iron, and fixes his teeth on the point. Already blood had begun to flow from his poisonous mouth and stained with its spray the green grass. But the wound was light, since he kept retreating from the blow, drawing his injured neck back, and by yielding kept fending off the blow, not allowing it to go further, until Cadmus, pursuing him, thrust the point in his throat, while an oak tree checked the serpent's retreat, and the neck and the oak were both impaled. The tree was bent by the weight of the serpent, and groaned that its wooden strength was lashed by the tip of his tail.

In the passage there are forty-two verbs: *dixit, sustulit, misit, mansit, reppulit, vicit, constitit, descendit, retorsit, adspexit, momordit, labefecit, eripuit, haesit, accessit, tumuerunt* (perfect, 59-73); *circumfluit, sonat, exit, inficit, cingitur, adstat, fertur, proturbat, cedit, sustinet, retardat, furit, dat, figit* (present, 74-84); *coeperat, tinxerat* (pluperfect, 85-86); *erat, retrahebat, dabat, arcebat, sinebat* (imperfect, 87-89); *pressit, obstitit, fixa est, curvata est, gemuit* (perfect, 90-94); fourteen present (33.3 percent), twenty-one perfect (50 percent), five imperfect (11.9 percent), and two pluperfect (4.7 percent).[1] These percentages tell us that, in contrast with his overall pattern (see Table 3, p. 35), Ovid is giving the perfect extra weight here—in fact, we have almost a reversal of his typical present/perfect ratio. This should warn us not to put too much weight on any single passage, but to try to discover the basic tendencies. What is more revealing about Ovid's method of storytelling here, in my opinion, is the way the present and perfect tenses are concentrated. The story begins in the perfect tense (fourteen and one-half lines), is continued in the present tense (eleven lines), and is concluded in the perfect tense (five lines). This is quite different from Vergil's use of the perfect tense to set his scenes, the present tense to portray the main action. Here the perfect does not seem to play the introductory or subordinate role that it does in the *Aeneid*. What we seem to have is an exciting narrative related first in the perfect, then in the present tense.

Our second passage from the *Metamorphoses* provides a further warning of the dangers of generalizing on the basis of a few lines, for it offers quite different statistics from the first. Nevertheless, its use of tense is quite different from Vergil's:

> sic fatus Cygnum repetit, nec fraxinus errat
> inque umero sonuit non evitata sinistro;
> inde velut muro solidaque a caute repulsa est.
> 125 qua tamen ictus erat, signatum sanguine Cygnum
> viderat et frustra fuerat gavisus Achilles:
> vulnus erat nullum, sanguis fuit ille Menoetae.
> tum vero praeceps curru fremebundus ab alto
> desilit et nitido securum comminus hostem
> 130 ense petens parmam gladio galeamque cavari
> cernit et in duro laedi quoque corpore ferrum.
> haut tulit ulterius clipeoque adversa retecti
> ter quater ora viri, capulo cava tempora pulsat
> cedentique sequens instat turbatque ruitque
> 135 attonitoque negat requiem: pavor occupat illum,
> ante oculosque natant tenebrae retroque ferenti
> aversos passus medio lapis obstitit arvo;
> quem super inpulsum resupino corpore Cygnum
> vi multa vertit terraeque adflixit Achilles.
> 140 tum clipeo genibusque premens praecordia duris
> vincla trahit galeae, quae presso subdita mento

elidunt fauces et respiramen utrumque
eripiunt animae. victum spoliare parabat;
arma relicta videt: corpus deus aequoris albam
contulit in volucrem, cuius modo nomen habebat.   145
                                                  (XII, 122-145)

So speaking, he renews his attack on Cygnus, and the ash spear does not miss its mark; unerring it rang out on his left shoulder, then rebounded from it as from a wall or solid rock. But Achilles had seen Cygnus marked with blood where he had been struck, and had rejoiced—in vain; there was no wound, and the blood was Menoetes'. Then indeed he leaps headlong from the lofty chariot with a roar; with gleaming sword he attacks his fearless foe in close combat, sees shield and helmet run through by his sword, but the iron itself broken on that unyielding flesh. He could bear no more; three times, four times he strikes his unprotected opponent in the face with a shield and on his hollow temples with sword hilt. The one retreats, the other, following, pursues him, drives him, overwhelms him and allows him no time to recover from his confusion. Fear seizes Cygnus, dark shadows swim before his eyes; a stone blocked his way as he retreated backward and he is hurled over it on his back. Achilles threw Cygnus down with great violence and dashed him to the ground. Then pressing on his chest with his shield and sturdy knees he draws tight the ties of his helmet, which press beneath his chin and crush his throat and cut off all passage of air. He was preparing to strip his victim—he sees abandoned armor. The god of the sea changed Cygnus into cygnet, the white bird whose name was recently his.

This passage contains twenty-nine verbs: *repetit, errat* (present, 122); *sonuit, repulsa est* (perfect, 123-24); *ictus erat, viderat, fuerat gavisus* (pluperfect, 125-26); *erat* (imperfect, 127); *fuit* (perfect, 127); *desilit, cernit* (present, 129-31); *tulit* (perfect, 132); *pulsat, instat, turbat, ruit, negat, occupat, natant* (present, 133-36); *obstitit, vertit, adflixit* (perfect, 137-39); *trahit, elidunt, eripiunt* (present, 140-43); *parabat* (imperfect, 143); *videt* (present, 144); *contulit* (perfect, 145) *habebat* (imperfect, 145); fifteen present (51.7

percent), eight perfect (27.6 percent), three imperfect and three
pluperfect (10.3 percent each). This fits more or less into Ovid's
overall pattern, although the percentage of perfects is a little low
and of pluperfects a little high. The pattern here is clearly different
from what we observed in Book III. This passage is, indeed, closer
to Vergil's narrative style than the other, for the present tense is
more important and tells more of the story, while the perfect verbs,
though not used just as Vergil uses his, do seem to play a more
introductory role than those in the other passage. In line 132, for
example, the perfect *haut tulit ulterius* introduces the action by
giving Achilles' emotional reaction to what has occurred, and the
next five verbs in the present tense depict his actions. But the scene
as a whole is different from a Vergilian scene, partly because there
are fewer verbs in the present tense, largely, I think, because of the
tense fluctuation (thirteen changes of tense in twenty-four lines),
which is quite different from what we normally find in Vergil. In
the Ovid passage, the tenses seem to set each other off to create a
vivid and varied picture, but one which is quite different from a
carefully constructed Vergilian scene where the present tense
seems imperceptibly to draw the reader into the narrative present.

These few observations will have to suffice for Ovid. It is time
to move on to Lucan and see what can be determined about the
tenses used in the *Pharsalia*.

> prima dies belli cessauit Marte cruento
> 25 spectandasque ducum uires numerosaque signa
> exposuit. piguit sceleris; pudor arma furentum
> continuit, patriaeque et ruptis legibus unum
> donauere diem; prono cum Caesar Olympo
> in noctem subita circumdedit agmina fossa,
> 30 dum primae perstant acies, hostemque fefellit
> et prope consertis obduxit castra maniplis.
> luce nova collem subito conscendere cursu,
> qui medius tutam castris dirimebat Ilerdam,
> imperat. huc hostem pariter terrorque pudorque
> 35 inpulit, et rapto tumulum prior agmine cepit.
> his uirtus ferrumque locum promittit, at illis
> ipse locus. miles rupes oneratus in altas
> nititur, aduersoque acies in monte supina

haeret et in tergum casura umbone sequentis
erigitur. nulli telum uibrare uacauit,   40
dum labat et fixo firmat uestigia pilo,
dum scopulos stirpesque tenent atque hoste relicto
caedunt ense uiam. uidit lapsura ruina
agmina dux equitemque iubet succedere bello
munitumque latus laeuo praeducere gyro.
sic pedes ex facili nulloque urguente receptus,   45
inritus et uictor subducto Marte pependit.

                                                            (IV, 24-47)

The first day of the war was free of bloody fighting; it set forth
to view the strength of the leaders and the numbers of their
troops. They repented their crime, shame checked the arms of
their frenzy and they granted their country and the laws they
had broken one day's grace. As the skies turned toward night,
Caesar surrounded his troops with a quickly-dug ditch, the
front lines standing fast, and he deceived the enemy, conceal-
ing his camp with troops drawn up closely together. At first
light he orders his men, at quick march, to climb the hill,
which, by its central location, separated Ilerda and kept it safe
from the camp. But fear and shame drove their enemy [the
Pompeians] to the same goal, and they took the hill first, after
hurried march. Valor and steel promise the place to Caesar's
men, their possession of it promises it to Pompey's. The
heavy-laden soldiers struggle up the high rocks, bent backwards; they cling to the cliff before them in battle formation,
kept from falling backwards by the shields of those behind.
None was free to throw his weapon, as they stagger and stick
their javelins in to support their steps, as they grasp rocks and
stumps, and cut a path with their swords, oblivious to the
enemy. Their leader saw that his troops would collapse, and
orders the cavalry to come to their assistance in battle, to
wheel to the left and interpose their left side. Thus the
infantry was saved easily and with no pusuit, while, the
fighting over, the victor lingered, having accomplished
nothing.

There are twenty-six verbs: *cessauit, exposuit, piguit, continuit
donauere, circumdedit* (perfect, 24-29); *perstant* (present, 30);

fefellit, obduxit (perfect, 30-31); *dirimebat* (imperfect, 33); *imperat* (present, 34); *inpulit, cepit* (perfect, 35); *promittit, nititur, haeret, erigitur* (present, 36-40); *uacauit* (perfect, 40); *labat, firmat, tenent, caedunt* (present, 41-43); *uidit* (perfect, 43); *iubet* (present, 44); *receptus, pependit* (perfect, 46-47); eleven (42.3 percent) in the present tense, fourteen (53.8 percent) in the perfect, one (3.8 percent) in the imperfect. These figures do not reflect the generalized statistics precisely (just as those from Ovid did not); we notice here, for example, that the present is significantly lower and the perfect significantly higher than the average (above, p. 35). These lines do, however, illustrate very clearly *how* Lucan puts a passage together. The first striking feature is the rapid alternation of tense: in twenty-four lines, eleven changes. There may be passages in the *Aeneid* with such fluctuation; it is certainly not Vergil's usual practice. Furthermore, although the perfect predominates, it does not do so as emphatically as the present tense normally does in the *Aeneid*. There, we remember, close to two—thirds of all narrative verbs are in the present tense and roughly one-quarter in the perfect; here, just over half are in the perfect and about two-fifths in the present—not so large a discrepancy. Still further, there does not seem to be any visible principle underlying Lucan's distribution of present and perfect. We might, at first, be tempted to generalize that if there is a chief narrative tense it must be the perfect. The first eight lines, for instance, are basically in the perfect (apart from one present—*dum perstant*—and since *dum* generally takes the present in Latin, one does not feel that it interrupts the perfects very noticeably). Next, however, there is a seven-and-one-half-line sequence (36-43) composed entirely of present verbs except for *uacauit* in the perfect (40). (A different way of regarding the latter part of this sequence would be to assume a tense change at *uacauit* which carries on through *uidit* (43), reading the present tenses with *dum* as grammatically necessary and therefore not chosen for effect.) The possibility that comes quite forcefully to mind is that the real principle underlying Lucan's choice of tense is variety. Norden's remark about the tendency of Latin to mix present and past tenses seems particularly apt when applied to Lucan.

Let us now look at our second passage:

ergo hostes portis, quas omnis soluerat urbis
cum fato conuersa fides, murisque recepti   705
praecipiti cursu flexi per cornua portus
ora petunt pelagusque dolent contingere classi.
heu pudor, exigua est fugiens uictoria Magnus.
angustus puppes mittebat in aequora limes
artior Euboica, qua Chalcida uerberat, unda.   710
hic haesere rates geminae, classique paratae
excepere manus, tractoque in litora bello
hic primum rubuit ciuili sanguine Nereus,
cetera classis abit summis spoliata carinis:
ut, Pagasaea ratis peteret cum Phasidos undas,   715
Cyaneas tellus emisit in aequora cautes;
rapta puppe minor subducta est montibus Argo
uanaque percussit pontum Symplegas inanem
et statura redit. iam Phoebum urguere monebat
non idem Eoi color aetheris, albaque nondum   720
lux rubet et flammas propioribus eripit astris,
et iam Plias hebet, flexi iam plaustra Bootae
in faciem puri redeunt languentia caeli,
maioresque latent stellae, calidumque refugit
Lucifer ipse diem. pelagus iam, Magne, tenebas,   725
non ea fata ferens quae cum super aequora toto
praedonem sequerere mari: lassata triumphis
desciuit Fortuna tuis, cum coniuge pulsus
et natis totosque trahens in bella penates
uadis adhuc ingens populis comitantibus exul.   730
quaeritur indignae sedes longinqua ruinae.
non quia te superi patrio priuare sepulchro
maluerint, Phariae busto damnantur harenae:
parcitur Hesperiae, procul hoc et in orbe remoto
abscondat Fortuna nefas, Romanaque tellus   735
inmaculata sui seruetur sanguine Magni.

(II, 704-36)

And so the enemy are admitted within the walls through the
gates, all of which the city had opened, its loyalty changed as
fortunes changed, and head for the shore in great haste,
following the branching arms of the harbor, lamenting that

the sea is available for the fleet. For shame—Pompey in flight is too small a victory! There was a narrow channel which admitted ships to the sea, narrower than that where Euboean waves beat on Chalcis. Here two ships stuck and bands of men in waiting for the fleet took them. Battle was moved to shore, and here first the sea grew red with the blood of civil war. The rest of the fleet sail off, robbed of its hindmost ships, just as the Argo got away from the rocks diminished only by the loss of its stern, when that ship from Pagasae was headed for the waves of Phasis and earth sent forth to the sea the Cyanean rocks—the clashing rocks in vain struck the empty sea and rebounded to stand still. Now the changed color of the eastern sky was warning of the imminence of Phoebus' daylight, the light, not yet white, glows ruddy and steals their fire from the nearer stars. Now Pleiades grow dull, now the wagon of curving Bootes, dimming gradually, merges into the face of clear sky, and Lucifer himself flees day's heat. By this time, Pompey, you were on the high sea, but without that good luck that was yours when you went after pirates over all the seas. Tired of your triumphs, Fortune deserted you. Driven out with wife and sons, drawing your whole household into battle, you go, an exile, still mighty in your entourage of nations. A distant site is sought for your undeserved downfall. The sands of Pharos are condemned to be your tomb, not because the gods above preferred to deprive you of a grave in your own country, but to spare Italy. Let Fortune conceal the crime far away in a distant region, and let Roman soil be kept unspotted by the blood of her great Pompey.

The incidence of tenses here is as follows: *soluerat* (pluperfect, 704); *petunt, dolent, est* (present, 707-08); *mittebat* (imperfect,709); *uerberat* (present, 710); *haesere, excepere, rubuit* (perfect, 711-13); *abit* (present, 714); *emisit, subducta est, percussit* (perfect, 716-18); *redit* (present, 719); *monebat* (imperfect, 719); *rubet, eripit, hebet, redeunt, latent* (present, 721-24); *refugit* (perfect, 724); *tenebas* (imperfect, 725); *desciuit* (perfect, 728); *uadis, quaeritur* (present, 730-31); *damnantur, parcitur* (present, 733-34). This passage offers statistics which, at first glance seem somewhat closer to those derived from the *Aeneid:* fifteen verbs (55.6 percent) in the present tense; eight (29.6 percent) in the perfect; three (11.1 percent) in the imperfect, and one (3.7 percent) in the pluperfect. Here, in contrast to the other passage, it is the present that is clearly the main narrative tense, as in Vergil. Unlike Vergil, however, Lucan shows the same rapid shifts in tense that we noticed before: here fourteen changes in thirty-three lines (not counting subjunctives), there eleven in twenty-four. Moreover, though statistically the chief narrative tense, the present does not assume this role with the same emphasis in Lucan as in Vergil, because Lucan does not seem to make a patterned use of it. Variety, again, seems to be the principle of choice, even more dramatically than in the lines from Book IV. What we seem to have is a story of past events told randomly in present and perfect with no substantial division of function; thus the effect is different from Vergil's treatment of his "scenes" in the present tense with transitional and subordinate information relegated to the perfect. In Lucan, at least in this small sampling, neither tense is made to carry the main narrative weight.

NOTES

Abbreviations Used in the Notes

AUTHORS

Anderson, *Art*

William S. Anderson, *The Art of the Aeneid* (Englewood Cliffs, 1969)

Anderson, "Iliad"

———, "Vergil's Second Iliad,"*TAPA* 88, 1957, 17-30.

Anderson, *Metamorphoses*

———, *Ovid's Metamorphoses*, Books 6-10 (Norman, 1972).

Conington

John Conington, *The Works of Virgil with a Commentary* (Hildesheim, 1963). Vol. 1, with Nettleship, rev. Haverfield; Vol. 2, rev. Nettleship; Vol. 3, rev. Nettleship.

Klingner, *Geisteswelt*

Friedrich Klingner, Römische Geisteswelt (Munchen, 1961).

Klingner, *Georgica*

———, *Virgils Georgica* (Zürich und Stuttgart, 1963).

Page

T.E. Page, ed., *The Aeneid*, Books I-VI, Books VII-XII (London, 1894, 1900).

Putnam, *Pastoral*

Michael C. J. Putnam, *Virgil's Pastoral Art, Studies in the Eclogues* (Princeton, 1970).

Putnam, *Poetry*

———, *The Poetry of the Aeneid, Four Studies in Imaginative Unity and Design* (Cambridge, Mass., 1965).

Quinn, *L.E.*

Kenneth Quinn, *Latin Explorations, Critical Studies in Roman Literature* (London, 1963).

Quinn, *V.A.*

Servius

Stolz-Schmalz

———, *Virgil's Aeneid, A Critical Description* (Ann Arbor, 1968). *Servii Grammatici Qui Feruntur in Vergilii Bucolica et Georgica Commentarii*, G. Thilo, ed. (Leipzig, 1887). *Servianorum In Vergilii Carmina Commentariorum* Editionis Harvardianae Volumen II, E.K. Rand et al., eds. (Lancaster, 1946); Volumen III, A.F. Stocker, A.H. Travis, eds. (Oxford, 1965). *Lateinische Grammatik*, Friedrich Stolz and J. H. Schmalz, eds., 5th ed., M. Leumann, J. Bapt. Hofmann, rev., Szantyr (München, 1963)

JOURNALS

AJP	*American Journal of Philology*
GRB	*Greek, Roman and Byzantine Studies*
HSCP	*Harvard Studies in Classical Philology*
MH	*Museum Helveticum*
RE	*Paulys Real-Encyclopädie der classischen Altertumswissenschaft*
TAPA	*Transactions and Proceedings of the American Philological Association.*

Notes to Chapter I

[1]See, for example, Hans Meyerhoff, *Time in Literature* (Berkeley, 1955); Madeleine Stein, "Counterclockwise: Flux of Time in Literature," *Sewanee Review* 44 (1936); and A. A. Mendilow, *Time and the Novel* (London, 1953), on modern literature. See Georges Poulet, *Studies in Human Time* (Baltimore, 1956), on French works from the medieval period and after, and Ricardo J. Quinones, *The Renaissance Discovery of Time* (Cambridge, Mass., 1972) on conceptions of time from Dante to Milton. See H. Fraenkel, "Die Zeitauffassung in der archaischen griechischen Literatur," *Wege und Formen frühgriechischen Denkens* (München, 1955), and Jacqueline de Romilly, *Time in Greek Tragedy* (Ithaca, 1968), on Greek literature. See Harry and Agathe Thornton, *Time and Style, A Psycho-Linguistic Essay in Classical Literature* (London, 1962), on Greek and Latin language and literature.

²See in particular A. O. Lovejoy and G. Boas, *Primitivism and Related Ideas in Antiquity* (Baltimore, 1935), and Bodo Gatz, *Weltalter, goldene Zeit und sinnverwandte Vorstellungen, Spudasmata XVI* (Hildesheim, 1967), on the Golden Age.

³See Julius Ley, *Vergilianarum Quaestionum De Temporum Usu* (Saarbrücken, 1877); Quinn, *L.E.*, 220-29, *V.A.*, 88-97; Michael von Albrecht, "Zu Vergils Erzähltechnik," *Glotta* 48 (1970) and his bibliography; and Anton Szantyr, "Bemerkungen zum Aufbau der Vergilischen Ekphrasis," *MH* 27 (1970).

⁴See Fraenkel (1955).

⁵See de Romilly (1968).

⁶de Romilly, 72-73.

⁷See chap. 4.

⁸This and all subsequent citations are from R.A.B. Mynors, ed., *P. Vergili Maronis Opera* (Oxford, 1969, repr. 1972).

⁹All translations are mine, intended to be clear and accurate rather than poetic. I am especially indebted to Allen Mandelbaum, *The Aeneid of Virgil* (New York, 1972), for help with the wording.

¹⁰W. A. Camps, in his book, *An Introduction to Virgil's Aeneid* (Oxford, 1969), discusses discrepancies and such in App. 3 and examines what he regards as imperfections of execution and design in App. 4. There are almost certainly some discrepancies in the poem, but I think that many of those he considers prove not to be discrepancies at all in the larger context of the poem. (See chap. 4, below.)

¹¹Thomas Greene, *The Descent from Heaven* (New Haven, 1963), p. 98.

¹²See App. 1.

¹³Consider the theme of exile, for example. The majority of principal characters and many others alluded to by Vergil—from Saturnus to Turnus—have had to flee their homelands and thus share a fundamental human experience.

¹⁴William Shakespeare, *The Tempest,* act 1, sc. 2. Cf. C.S. Lewis, *A Preface to Paradise Lost* (Oxford, 1942), p. 34.

¹⁵In connection with Sergius, it seems to me a nice touch to have the family responsible for the notorious Catiline descended from the man who foolhardily wrecks his ship in the race. In connection with the fourth captain, Gyas, Servius, vol. 3, states that he also fathered a Roman clan, the Gens Gegania. Vergil does not mention it, perhaps as A. Forbiger suggests (*P. Vergili Maronis Opera*, 4th ed. [Leipzig, 1873]), from feelings of delicacy, because the family had died out by Augustan times.

¹⁶See chap. 2, p. 24 and n. 24.

Notes to Chapter II

¹The best recent book on the *Eclogues* is probably *Vergil's Eclogues, Landscapes of Experience* (Ithaca, 1974), by Eleanor Winsor Leach, a book which has given *Eclogue* studies a new direction. It has changed my

thinking about the *Eclogues* in many ways and would doubtless have done so still more if it had come out before I finished my work on the poems. My observations on the *Eclogues* may seem somewhat slight after Leach's substantial treatment of the whole *Eclogue* book. I hope they will, nevertheless, accomplish their purpose, which is primarily to provide an introduction to Vergil's use of time in the *Aeneid*.

[2]Putnam, *Pastoral*, p. 258.

[3]G.W. Bowersock, "A Date in the *Eighth Eclogue*," *HSCP* 75 (1971), p. 79; Wendell Clausen, "On the Date of the First *Eclogue*," *HSCP* 76 (1972), pp. 201-5.

[4]See Putnam, *Pastoral*, chapter 1.

[5]Karl Büchner, *RE* 84, 1186; Klingner, *Geisteswelt*, pp. 278-79. But see Leach, p. 203 and n. 71, "Many echoes of the earlier poem (1) show that the pastoral life has become more precarious." "The point of these retrospective motifs is often obscured by those who think that the ninth poem was composed first and represents an initial attempt to save the farm, while the first poem represents a final success."

[6]Leach argues against the identification of the "god" with Octavian, pp. 126-30. William Berg, *Early Virgil* (London, 1974), in contrast, assumes as a matter of course that he is Octavian.

[7]Conington, vol. 1, *ad loc.*

[8]On the subject see Berg, pp. 164-65.

[9]See especially Zeph Stewart, "The Song of Silenus," *HSCP* 64 (1959), pp. 179-205, and J.P. Elder, "*Non iniussa cano*, Virgil's Sixth Eclogue," *HSCP* 65 (1961), pp. 109-25.

[10]*Reges et proelia* (line 3) may refer to epic in general, but historical epic is specifically rejected a few lines later, so it seems likely that mythological epic is at issue here.

[11]On Callimachus and Vergil see Wendell Clausen, "Callimachus and Latin Poetry," *GRB* 5, 1964, pp. 181-96.

[12]Brooks Otis, *Virgil*, [*A*] *Study in Civilized Poetry* (Oxford, 1963), chap. 2.

[13]Servius I.

[14]Hylas may well be instanced as an example of an epic theme already reworked (if we assume, with Gow—Preface to *Id.* 13 [A.S.F. Gow, *Theocritus*, Cambridge, 1950]—that Theocritus' version was a "correction" of Apollonius').

[15] "Disorder and chaos are no longer bound to historical causes, places, and times. Gallus takes his chaos with him, transcending place and time." Leach, p. 168.

[16]On the language see Putnam, *Pastoral*, chap. 9.

[17]For a comprehensive bibliography of the *Georgics*, see L.P. Wilkinson, *The Georgics of Virgil* (Cambridge, 1969), pp. 343-50.

[18]I cannot do justice to the *Georgics* here. I merely hope to point out a few things about Vergil's use of time in the poem that tie in with his practice in the *Aeneid*.

[19]*Hesiodi Theogonia, Opera et Dies, Scutum*, F. Solmsen, ed. (Oxford, 1970).

[20]For a slightly different view of the meaning of *labor,* see Heinrich Altevogt, *Labor Improbus, eine Vergilstudie* (Münster, 1952), pp. 9-10, whose interpretation of *vicit* accords with mine; for a different interpretation of *vicit,* see Klingner, *Georgica,* pp. 40-41; on *improbus,* see Otis, p. 157, n. 1.

[21]This is a technique that Vergil uses to stunning effect in the *Aeneid.* See chap. 3.

[22]Cf. Horace, Epode 7.

[23]I think Conington is mistaken when he says, vol. 1: "Virgil's allusion here to Troy seems purely learned and literary." I find the reference to Troy and Laomedon very suggestive.

[24]This poem (and its connection with the *Georgics*) was brought to my attention by Maynard Mack.

[25]See Otis, pp. 152ff, on the tone and pattern of the books of the *Georgics.*

[26]A. Forbiger, *P. Vergili Maronis Opera* (Leipzig, 1873 and 1875), *ad loc.*

[27]Forbiger thinks the words apply *only* to the young shoots. I disagree.

[28]It is no accident that Lucretius' great poem, *De Rerum Natura, On the Nature of Things,* comes to mind again and again as we read the *Georgics.* Both poems deal with the way things are, and Vergil frequently alludes to the earlier poet.

[29]Wilkinson, p. 91.

[30]Cf. *Eclogue* 3, 88-89:

> qui te, Pollio, amat, veniat quo te quoque gaudet;
> mella fluant illi, ferat et rubus asper amomum.

> Let him who loves you, Pollio, come where he is happy you too have come. Let honey flow for him, let the prickly bramble bear spices.

[31]It is possible that the reference is not to sacrifice, but only to vegetarianism. That is the view of F. Bowen, *P. Virgilii Maronis Bucolica, Georgica, et Aeneis* (Boston & Cambridge, 1858). A.O. Lovejoy and G. Boas, p. 32, refer it to sacrifice and vegetarianism.

[32]G.B. Miles, a friend and colleague at the University of California at Santa Cruz, suggested the parallel between opportunities lost to the past and opportunities lost to the future.

Notes to Chapter III

[1]Julius Ley (Saarbrücken, 1877).

[2]See chap. 1, n. 3.

[3]*L.E.,* p. 222.

[4]I am assuming that present tenses are chosen for stylistic reasons rather than from grammatical necessity. See Hermann Koller, "Praesens historicum und erzählendes Imperfekt," *MH* (1951), pp. 63-99. In his view, many historical presents in Plautus and Sallust (as well as in Greek authors) are chosen not for effect, but because the verbs in question lose their inceptive character in the perfect. The situation is different with Vergil. "Das Praesens historicum . . . ist rein stilistisches Mittel geworden", p. 86.

[5]*V.A.*, p. 89.

[6]*Allen and Greenough's New Latin Grammar*, J.B. Greenough, G. L. Kittredge, et al., eds. (Boston, 1903), p. 295.

[7]Eduard Norden, *P. Vergilius Maro Äneis Buch VI* (4th ed., Stuttgart, 1957), p. 113.

[8]*M. Annaei Lucani Belli Civilis Libri Decem*, A.E. Housman, ed. (Oxford, 1927).

[9]*P. Ovidius Naso, Metamorphosen*, M. Haupt, ed., rev., von Albrecht, Vol. I, 10th ed., Vol. II, 5th ed. (Zürich/Dublin, 1966).

[10]von Albrecht, p. 225.

[11]Norden, p. 113. Koller, pp. 83-84, comments on the alternation of speeches in the perfect, narrative in the present. In his view, continual alternation of present and perfect is colloquial.

[12]Ley, p. 9. Cf. von Albrecht, p. 220.

[13]Richard Heinze, *Virgils epische Technik* (5th ed., Stuttgart, 1965), p. 374.

[14]In the following discussion, my most important points have not, so far as I know, been set out elsewhere. Occasionally, my conclusions about the effect of a particular tense coincide with others'. Rather than take issue with every point, I have set out my views in one coherent statement, citing others only when their views seem most relevant to my argument.

[15]See Quinn, *L.E.*, pp. 223-26 on changes of tempo.

[16]These are coupled with imperfects, whose function will be examined later.

[17]Stolz-Schmalz, II, 315.

[18]Ley, p. 8. Cf. Quinn, *V.A.*, pp. 86-87.

[19]Quinn, *V.A.*, p. 94.

[20]See Norden *ad* VI, 523-25.

[21]Quinn, *L.E.*, p. 223.

[22]*P. Ovidius Naso, Die Fasten*, F. Bömer, ed., Band I (Heidelberg, 1957).

[23]Contrast Dryden's translation, "Once oxen low'd, where now the lawyers bawl." This is witty and very effective in its own way, but more suited to Ovid's lines, quoted above, p. 51, than to Vergil's here. Dryden separates what Vergil joined.

Notes to Chapter IV

[1]W.H. Auden, "Secondary Epic," *Homage to Clio* (New York, 1960), line 3.

[2]Furthermore, his elaborate purple and gold cloak and his beautiful

jeweled sword (more for looks than for use, it would seem) say a lot about his present situation and mood.

[3]Following MP I exclude line 273 *nec super ipse tua moliris laude laborem*. See Conington for arguments against the line. I would add to his explanation that it suits the prophetic context to leave out the reference to *labor*.

[4]The three verbs (present tense) representing three separate actions, the quick alternation of dactyls and spondees, the position of the caesura emphasizing the parallelism of *animum nunc huc* and *celerem nunc huc* contribute to the light, fast-paced effect of the lines in IV; while a weightier, more massive effect is created in V by the single static imperfect verb, the predominance of spondees, and the caesura emphasizing the parallelism of *nunc huc ingentis* and *nunc illuc curas*.

[5]See chap. 3, p. 39 for discussion.

[6]A. Cartault, *L'Art de Virgile dans L'Énéide* (Paris, 1926), p. 595.

[7]On Jupiter's prophecies, see below, pp. 77ff.

[8]"Ce qui est histoire dans l'Énéide, c'est le mouvement du récit épique; ce qui est mythe, c'est la vision de l'histoire," J.P. Brisson, "Temps Historique et Mythique dans l'Énéide," *Vergiliana*, H. Bardon, R. Verdiére, eds. (Leiden, 1971), p. 68.

[9]Auden, lines 1-5.

[10]See Livy, Book I, passim. *Titi Livi Ab Urbe Condita*, C.F. Walters, R.S. Conway, eds. (Oxford, 1919).

[11]No one has, so far as I know, been able to make anything of the fact that Ancus is here given characteristics traditionally given to Servius Tullius, who is not mentioned at all.

[12]Despite Norden (*ad loc.*), I agree with Conington that, in the Latin, *anima* is clearly linked with Brutus.

[13]The name Cato can suggest Cato, the Elder, as Heyne, Forbiger, and Conington think, as well as Cato, the Younger, regarded as the Stoic hero of the late Republic. The reference to the Gracchi probably implies the T. Sempronius Gracchus of the second Punic war or the father of the famous tribunes, or both, as well as the tribunes themselves.

[14]See Brisson, pp. 65-66.

[15]See Livy, VI, 19-20.

[16]Cf. M. E. Taylor, "Primitivism in Virgil," *AJP* 76 (1955), p. 267.

[17]With some reluctance I accept Mynor's reading *paci* for *pacis* because of the manuscript evidence. I am surprised that he makes no mention of the alternative and usual reading of one of the most famous passages in the poem.

[18]See, for example Otis, p. 215ff. and Quin, *V.A.*, p. 67ff.

[19]See C.M. Bowra, *From Virgil to Milton* (London, 1945), p. 38, for example, on Vergil's distaste for war and his difficulties in writing about it, or Heinze, p. 189, on the problems Vergil faced in dealing with his model addressed to "das schlachtenfrohe Publikum Homers." For more modern views, see, in particular, Otis, Quinn, *V.A.*, Anderson, *Art;* Steele Commager, pp. 1-13 and Adam Parry, "Two Voices in Vergil's Aeneid," *Virgil, A Collection of Critical Essays* (Englewood Cliffs, 1969).

[20]I, 19-22, 257-96, 389-401, 444-45; II, 293-95, 780-89; III, 41-46, 94-98, 154-71, 182-85, 250-57, 377-462, 539-43; IV: 265-76, 560-70; V, 728-37, 813-15; VI, 83-97, 756-886 (excluding 854 and 860-67); VII, 68-70, 79-80, 96-101, 124-27; VIII, 36-62, 626-728.

[21]IX, 641-44; X, 11-15, 241-45; XII, 832-40.

[22]When a prophecy is embedded in a speech, it is sometimes difficult to decide where the prophecy proper begins. When I was unsure, I defined as prophecy the lines that pertain to the future, including commands and present actions intended to bring about that future.

[23]macte noua uirtute, puer, sic itur ad astra,
dis genite et geniture deos. iure omnia bella
gente sub Assaraci fato uentura resident,
nec te Troia capit. . . .

Increase in bravery, boy, born of gods, destined to sire gods—that is the way to the stars. Rightfully shall all wars fated to come cease under the race of Assaracus, Troy cannot contain you.

[24]namque tibi reduces socios classemque relatam
nuntio et in tutum uersis Aquilonibus actam,
ni frustra augurium uani docuere parentes.

I report to you the return of your companions and fleet, driven to safety when the winds changed, unless my parents uselessly taught me augury in vain.

[25]"As the dreadful thing beats at the face of Turnus, his terror gathers into itself all the terrors that have preceded it: the unseen horror is at last physically present, and the daughter of darkness has become visible. . . . its special success derives from the emphasis on a peculiarly sinister quality that all the ministers of evil in the poem share and that surpasses even the brilliant imaginations of evil and madness that we find in Greek tragic choruses. What Turnus meets face to face, what evokes in him nightmarish impotence and despair, is not a traditional bogey cleverly magnified; it is rather a wild, vindictive negation of goodness, an active, gloating privation of goodness and being." W.R. Johnson, *Darkness Visible* (Berkeley, 1976), p. 147.

[26]Cf. Anderson, "Iliad."

[27]Cf. chap. 2, n. *23.*

[28]Cf. A.F. Lossev, "Les Mouvements Affectives dans l'Énéide," *Vergiliana.* p. 201. He concludes from this that Turnus' passion is a "fait du sort."

[29]Quinn, *V.A.*, pp. 211-12; Otis, pp. 345-51.

[30]It is my feeling that we are intended to regret Lausus even more than we regret Dido. Lausus seems to me to represent all that is young and innocent and good that is destroyed in warfare. Even the language used of

his exploits (427-30) detaches and abstracts him from the general slaughter (in contrast to Pallas, who loses to a stronger warrior only after fighting several fierce and bloody battles). Lausus' death results from his *pietas*, his sense of love and duty to his father. No duel, like that between Pallas and Turnus, takes place; Aeneas merely runs him through with terrible ease. It is possible to see Lausus' death almost as a crime, a murder in cold blood. Aeneas almost instantly regrets it and never really recovers from it.

[31]See Otis, p. 368, on Turnus' folly, and Frank O. Copley, *Latin Literature from the Beginnings to the Close of the Second Century A.D.* (Ann Arbor, 1969), pp. 231-32, on Aeneas' military blunder.

Notes to Chapter V

[1]See Johnson, chap. 1, for a recent survey of the main trends of Vergilian scholarship since T.S. Eliot.

[2]John L. Balderston, *Berkeley Square* (New York, 1929).

[3]Virginia Woolf, *Orlando* (New York, 1928).

[4]Mendilow, p. 99-100.

[5]*Prometheus*, 981; *Aeschyli Septem Quae Supersunt Tragodiae*, D. Page, ed. (Oxford, 1972).

[6]Contrast the similes used of Turnus and those used of Aeneas. Ten of the fifteen similes associated with Turnus depict animals. This is obvious and often commented upon. Many of the sixteen centering on Aeneas, however, have to do with rather more sinister comparisons, with relentless and impassive forces far more deadly than any beast: storms, fires, rivers, the crash of thunder, Sirius, and even Aegaeon. Aegaeon (or Briareus) is the hundred-handed monster who traditionally aided Zeus against the Titans. Vergil has him fight *against* Jupiter. Little attention has been paid to the similes of this sort connected with Aeneas. They seem to me very suggestive.

Notes to Appendix I

[1]Quintilian IX, 3, 62, *M. Fabi Quintiliani Institutionis Oratoriae Libri Duodecim*, M. Winterbottom, ed. (Oxford, 1970), defines zeugma as a figure in which several clauses, each of which would need a verb if alone, are attached to a single verb *(in qua unum ad uerbum plures sententiae referuntur, quarum unaquaeque desideraret illud si sola poneretur).* There does not appear to be any early definition of hendiadys. According to the *Oxford English Dictionary*, it first appears in Servius. It does not seem to be mentioned in the Greek rhetorical writers where we might expect to find it.

[2]Ovid has done better for himself. Anderson, *Metamorphoses*, has a number of useful and suggestive comments on zeugma as well as on other aspects of Ovid's poetry.

[3]On this passage see Greene, p. 98.

[4]All the commentators I have consulted translate this "up from the ocean," which seems a reasonable translation except that I have been unable to find any phrase (including those they cite) in which *ruo* clearly implies motion upward.

[5]I have not made a complete study of zeugma in Latin poetry (although I have in progress an essay on it) and I cannot claim that Vergil's use of the figure is unique. It does seem to be characteristic of him and different, at least, from Ovid's typical practice. Very frequently in Ovid, as in the following example:

.... at illi
et mens et quod opus fabrilis dextra tenebat
excidit. . . .

Meta. IV, 174-76

but both his spirits and the work his craftsman's hand was holding fell,

the zeugma undercuts the gravity of the situation (in this case the discovery by Vulcan that his lovely wife Venus is committing adultery) and introduces an element of wit into the poem. In this Ovid resembles Alexander Pope, as, for example, in the *Rape of the Lock:*

Here Thou, Great Anna! whom three Realms obey,
Dost sometimes Counsel take—and sometimes *Tea.*

Canto III, lines 7-8

This sort of zeugma is quite different from Vergil's. Vergil's zeugmatic linkings are generally aimed less at wit or humor than economy. They help to pack extra meaning into a group of words.

[6]Cf. Servius, *ad loc.*

[7]Similar is the famous zeugma that opens Tacitus' *Germania:* Germania omnis a Gallis Raetisque et Pannoniis Rheno et Danuuio fluminibus, a Sarmatis Dacisque mutuo metu aut montibus separatur.

(*P. Cornelii Taciti Libri Qui Supersunt,* Erich Koestermann, ed., Tom. II, Fasc. 2, Leipzig, 1964.)

All Germany is separated from the Gauls, Raetians and Pannonians by the Rhine and Danube rivers, from the Sarmatians and Dacians by mutual fear or mountains.

Notes to Appendix II

[1]See pp. 33-34 for the principles underlying my verb counts.

GENERAL INDEX

Aeneas: depicted as Achilles, Hector, Paris, Laomedon's heir, 80-81; disintegrations in, 82-83; receives "directional" prophecies, 56-67; shield of, 72-75; similes for, 115 n6; war of, 78-79, 80-84, 88.
Aeschylus, 3.
Anchises, 5-6, 62. *See also* prophecy.
Apollonius, 2-3; used by Vergil in *Eclogues,* 15.
Auden, W.H., 112 n1, 113 n9.
Augustus, 71-72.
Balderston, J.L., 86.
Brutus, 70.
Caesar, 70-71.
Callimachus, 14, 15.
Catullus, 64, 13-14.
Dante, 87.
Dryden, 112 n23.
Eclogues: Gallus and elegy in, 16-18; myth and history in, 5; pastoral timelessness and historical time in, 4, 7-14; pastoral and epic in, 11-16.
Future; disappearance of in *Aen.* IX-XII, 76-80; immediate, 56; long range, 56. *See also* prophecy.
Gallus, 15-18, 28.
Georgics: encomium of spring, 25-27; juxtaposition of times, 21-22; *Laudes Italiae:* Golden Age ease and progressive

civilization, 24-25; merging of present and past, 18-21, 25-27; movement through time, 4. *See also* Golden Age.
Golden Age: in *Aeneid,* 5, 69, 71, 72, 74, 75, 87; in *Eclogues,* 11-13, 111 n30; in *Georgics,* 18-21, 24-25, 27-30.
Hendiadys, 89-91, 93.
Hesiod, 18, 31.
Iliad, 2, 80.
Iron Age, 19-21.
Justice, 28, 29, 30.
Keats, 83.
Laomedon, *Laomedonteus,* 22, 81, 111 n3.
Livy, 49.
Lucan, 35, 36, 48, 49, 95, 100-5.
Manlius (Marcus Manlius Capitolinus), 73-74.
Marcellus, 71-72.
Mettus, 73.
Mezentius, 76, 82.
Octavian. *See* Augustus.
Odyssey, 2, 5, 15.
Ovid, 35, 36, 48, 49, 51.
Past. *See* Tenses.
Patterning, 5, 18, 31, 39ff., 48, 95ff.
Pollio, 11-12.
Pompey, 70-71.
Poussin, 9.
Present: nature of in *Aen.* IX-XII, 80-84; relation of to past in *Aen.* IX- XII, 80, 81. *See also* tenses.

117

INDEX OF PASSAGES

The following entries are alphabetical by author. To the left of each, in italics, are the works and passages cited in the text; to the right are the pages on which they occur.

119